D0075648

The King's Parliament of England

Historical Controversies • A Norton Series

Under the general editorship of BRYCE LYON, *Brown University*

The King's
Parliament
of England

by G. O. Sayles

D. Litt., Litt. D., Fellow of the British Academy

W · W · Norton & Company · Inc · New York

Copyright © 1974 by W. W. Norton & Company, Inc.
FIRST EDITION

All Rights Reserved
Published simultaneously in Canada
by George J. McLeod Limited, Toronto

Library of Congress Cataloging in Publication Data

Sayles, George Osborne, 1901–
   The King's Parliament of England.
   (Historical controversies)
   Bibliography: p.
   1. Legislative bodies—Great Britain—History. 2. Great Britain. Parliament—History. I. Title. II. Series.
JN515.S35   328.42′09   74–95544
ISBN 0–393–05508–6
ISBN 0–393–09322–0 (pbk.)

FOR
Michael AND *Hilary*

Contents

Foreword

This short book had its origins in 1967 when I made the king's parliament in medieval England the subject of an Inaugural Address I delivered as Kenan Professor of History at New York University and was invited thereafter by Professor Bryce Lyon of Brown University to contribute to this series. I welcome the opportunity to summarise the conclusions reached with Mr. H. G. Richardson in many articles in learned periodicals over forty years. Often we projected and, indeed, made final arrangements for the publication of a comprehensive and detailed history of parliament, but other interests persistently intervened. Much, however, was written that will not see the light of day and I am indebted to Mr. Richardson for permission to draw upon it. My commitment was to explain the origins and early development of parliament, but there is no proper stopping place before the Long Parliament of the Reformation in 1529, which brought the Middle Ages, so far as constitutional history is concerned, to an end. I have therefore been kindly permitted to go beyond my allotted space and add a final chapter of reflections on the place of parliament in the late fourteenth and fifteenth centuries. Although the book is based on much material that has never been printed, references have been cut to a minimum, though a few documents are cited where the reader can rightly call for the production of proof. Hard experience has taught me that it is impossible to destroy a national myth, in England or in any

other country. When I read recent textbooks on history and
law, I cannot even share the optimism of Max Planck in his
final testimony: 'A new scientific truth does not triumph by
convincing its opponents and making them see the light but
rather because its opponents eventually die and a new genera-
tion grows up that is familiar with it' (A *Scientific Autobiog-
raphy*, trans. 1950, pp. 33f.). But if this Pisgah view can make
it easier for the inexperienced to question rather than accept,
it will have served some purpose.

Warren Hill　　　　　　　　　　　　　　　　　　G. O. S.
Crowborough
Sussex
2 September 1973

Classification of Manuscripts

Public Record Office, London

C. 49   Chancery, Parliament and Council Proceedings
C. 54   Close Rolls
C. 65   Chancery Parliament Rolls
C. 66   Patent Rolls

E. 159   Exchequer, King's Remembrancer's
                Memoranda Rolls
E. 163   Exchequer Miscellanea
E. 175   Exchequer, Parliament and Council Proceedings
E. 368   Exchequer, Lord Treasurer's Remembrancer's
                Memoranda Rolls

J. I. 1   Assize Rolls, Eyre Rolls, etc.

K. B. 26   Curia Regis Rolls
K. B. 27   King's Bench Rolls

S. C. 1   Ancient Correspondence
S. C. 8   Ancient Petitions
S. C. 9   Exchequer Parliament Rolls

The King's Parliament of England

1. Modern Myths
and Medieval Parliaments

Just as today we remember Athens and Rome not
so much for their transient empires as for their permanent
contributions to art, philosophy, and jurisprudence, so England,
now bereft of empire, will remain honoured for its development of the common law, which spread over half the world,
and for its political experimentations, which eventually produced a workable democracy. These two developments cannot
be rigidly separated, for they were constantly interacting, as we
hope to demonstrate, but it is with the genesis and early
history of parliament that we are particularly concerned. Parliamentary institutions we are apt to regard as something pecu-
liarly English, the creation of centuries of trial and error, and
closely related to the administrative structure of England itself.
It is true that in the past hundred years or so they have been
adopted by other than English-speaking peoples, both within
Europe and outside it. But this has entailed a grafting of something new and alien onto an old stock and, as we plainly see,
the results have been far from uniformly successful. Why there
should be failures, why sometimes parliamentarianism should
have had only a partial success, and why men should revolt
against it: these are not matters for us to answer here. Yet it
may help us with our answers, difficult as they are to give, if
we understood how parliaments arose in England and how
they developed. Not that history has ever any direct lesson for

us, but it alone has the merit of helping us to ask the right questions by placing them in some sort of perspective.

We are first concerned with modern arguments about the medieval parliament. When we say 'modern', we do not mean simply the historians of our own day but the long line of historians reaching back into and even before the early seventeenth century, with men like Edward Coke and John Selden, William Blackstone and William Stubbs. Nevertheless, we for our part will be mainly trying to commune with the men of the Middle Ages themselves in the belief that the truth for which historians must search is the contemporary truth, that the men of the time knew best what the real purpose of the medieval parliament was in the governance of the realm. Of course, they did not know what would come to matter most to later ages. But they did know what mattered most to themselves. Now, it is at our peril that we confuse these two things. If we concentrate on what matters to us today we teeter on the edge of propaganda, and emphasis of this kind certainly brought about the creation of the modern myth of the medieval parliament. But if we prefer history to propaganda, we must stress what mattered to contemporaries. Since this often goes counter to the orthodox legends, it is likely to be stigmatised as heresy, though it is still true that if a scientific man has not learned to be heretical, he has learned nothing. In other words, the very basis of history, like that of science, is always scepticism and never acceptance. We must not expose ourselves to the scathing satire of a French novelist [1] which we cannot forbear to quote, though in translation: 'Why compose a history book when all you have to do is to copy the best-known ones, as is the custom? If you have a new view, an original idea, if you exhibit men and things in an unexpected light, you will surprise the reader. And the reader does not like to be surprised. He looks in a history book for the legends he knows already. If you try to teach him, you will do nothing but humiliate him and annoy him. Do not try to enlighten him or he will exclaim that you are attacking his beliefs. So copy one another and thereby save yourselves fatigue and avoid appearing bumptious (*outre-cuidant*).'

1. Anatole France.

We may be allowed a simple illustration. Edward I, once the imagined architect of an imaginary parliament, was said many years ago to have faithfully observed his motto of *pactum serva*, that is, 'keep your obligations', though we should add that to many of his contemporaries he seemed both in youth and old age a double-crosser, a liar, and a cheat. And still today one historian will assert that Edward's motto was to 'keep troth'; another will make him apply it in practice; a third will depict him as proud to possess it. And yet there is no contemporary evidence for this motto: the words *pactum serva* were carved upon Edward's tomb in Westminster Abbey not in his own day but two hundred and fifty years after his death; the king and the motto had nothing to do with one another.[2]

In recounting the history of the early parliaments of England, and, in particular, the minor part played in them by the representatives of the people, we are conscious that it will seem a strange one to many who read it. Our explanation must be, as we have said, that we have tried to look at parliament through the eyes of men of the thirteenth, fourteenth, and fifteenth centuries. Of course, none of us who live in the twentieth century can achieve this with anything approaching complete success: we cannot place ourselves altogether on the eye-level of medieval man. And we are further hampered in our task by the natural pride we take in our past, for we like to believe that our thoughts, our liberties, our beliefs were those also of our fathers and have come to us in their original integrity. And so, by an inversion of history, we make our ancestors speak our language, conduct themselves by our own standards, pursue our own ends. But the three Edwards who sat successively on the English throne from 1272 onward, Simon de Montfort and Thomas of Lancaster, their servants, their friends and supporters, stand far removed from us in ideas, speech, and aims. And then a further fallacy supervenes, against which a wise warning was given many years ago: 'Knowing what did happen, by a kind of historical fatalism we assume that it was the only thing which could have happened. More than this, we assume that everything which did not obviously help it to

2. A. P. Stanley, *Historical Memorials of Westminster Abbey*, p. 119, n. 4, p. 402.

happen may be relegated to a limbo of things which themselves only half happened'. [3] So we come to imagine, and try to prove, not only that the roots of all our institutions are in the past—as must, indeed, be true—but that at a time when the seed was barely sown the plant was already flowering.

Now, the history of the medieval parliament of England has been seriously distorted by both these assumptions. The history of parliament was not originally studied for its own sake. Indeed, if that had been attempted, it would have been dismissed as useless and valueless. Early writers on this subject in the seventeenth century were not detached observers who were willing to let the story tell itself. They were not so much interested in what had happened in the past as in what they themselves considered to matter; and what mattered to them was that they should find similarities in the past by which their policies could be guided and their actions justified in the current political debate whether king alone or king and parliament together was to be supreme. They could not see that the constitutional controversies were not those also of the Middle Ages and that the problem of sovereignty had never been posed in the form in which it appeared in their own day. The parliament of the Middle Ages was for them the same institution as the parliament of the seventeenth century. The concept of evolution, of incessant change, of breaks in continuity, which we nowadays accept as a commonplace of thought, lay still far in the future. Scholars like Sir Thomas Smith and Sir Henry Spelman, Coke and Selden, Petyt and Brady, even Blackstone, had not heard of evolution and they thought not in terms of continuous creation but of instantaneous acts of creation, not of historical relativity but of the immutability of institutions. *In saecula saeculorum:* as it was in the beginning, is now, and ever shall be. Archbishop Ussher, an early seventeenth-century scholar whose erudition few today can match, could see no absurdity in his calculation that the world had been created all at once in 4004 B.C. on 23 October at nine o'clock in the morning.[4] As with Ussher and the earth, so with historians and parliament: an all-wise legislator had created a model parliament, and it seemed safe at one time to

3. A. L. Smith, *Church and State in the Middle Ages*, p. 5.
4. J. B. Bury, *History of Freedom of Thought*, p. 143.

ascribe the handiwork to one man, Edward I, the English Justinian, to use the seventeenth-century phrase, and even to give it a date: 1295. And a book on parliament, published not so many years ago, has in fact as its title A *Short History of Parliament,* 1295–1642.[5]

So these early scholars, exhibiting a grand disregard for the passage of time and the alteration of circumstance, compelled the past to reflect the present. And having put the seventeenth century into the Middle Ages before they began to look for it, they had, of course, no difficulty in finding it there. The passage of centuries meant to them no such discontinuity as we feel, especially nowadays, in quite a brief passage of years. Indeed, most of them were lawyers or men who were daily breathing a legal atmosphere, and common lawyers have little or no sense of time. When John Hampden was prosecuted in 1636 for not paying the taxation called ship-money, both sides saw nothing incongruous in citing evidence from the reign of King Egbert, 802–39. So they selected evidence to agree with their tendentious assumptions. Since they wrote nothing on parliament that did not have a political purpose, this purpose fixed the choice of documents to support their theses. Out of the great mass of evidence that then existed, and still exists today, they chose to concentrate their attention solely on writs of summons and rolls of parliament, for these suited their conceptions of parliament. This choice of material, made in the seventeenth century, determined for all time the general form and content of later compilations of parliamentary records, and that choice by itself has carried its bias with it unnoticed down the ages. Thus the three main collections of documents in print—the *Rolls of Parliament* (1783), the *Parliamentary Writs* (1827–34) in four massive folio volumes, the *Lords Reports on the Dignity of a Peer* (1820–29) with its copious appendix of documents, inevitably writs of summons —add little or nothing to what was already known to seventeenth-century scholars. Printing merely made the information more accessible.

Let us illustrate this habit of mind from a book which had no very obtrusive controversial intention, Henry Elsynge's *Manner of Holding Parliaments in England,* written in 1625 but not

5. Faith Thompson (Minnesota Univ. Press, 1953).

published until 1660. This was intended to be a practical man-
ual on parliamentary procedure, and it is clear that a precedent
from the reign of Edward III or earlier corresponds in authority with a precedent from the reign of Elizabeth.[6] Past and
present were alike and Elsynge has no apprehension that in the
thirteenth and fourteenth centuries he has to do with an institution widely different from the parliament which he himself
served as clerk, and that precedents drawn from utterly different societies and ways of thought have only a tenuous validity.

Nothing is now less likely to stir our passions than a collection of parliamentary writs of summons. But, although William Prynne spoke of their 'manifold, rare, delightful varieties,
forms and diversities', we should hardly expect them to 'become like to the leaves of the tree of life' or to assist in making
'our future parliaments beneficial, medicinal and restorative to
our nation'.[7] Nor should we expect that they would instruct
'ignoramusses in parliamentary procedure',[8] if by that we
meant, as he meant, members of parliament who had done
something of which we disapproved. Prynne we may regard
as an eccentric: he was certainly a violent, quarrelsome fellow,
who found apposite any argument drawn from his vast learning,
and, like so many of his fellows, he pulled no punches.

But what of his contemporary, another antiquarian, William
Dugdale? He, like Prynne, was interested mainly in the composition of parliament and he ignored the mass of evidence on
the chancery rolls alone which would have told him the purposes parliament served. In 1685 he published with a very brief
preface 675 pages of what we should regard as a quite unexciting
*Perfect Copy of the Summons of the Nobility to the Great
Councils and Parliaments of This Realm from the XLIX of
King Henry the III[d]*. Dugdale was far from finding his writs of
summons unexciting. Here was evidence, he claimed, 'that the
Great Councils of the Nation, commonly called Parliaments,
. . . were always convened by the kings of this realm. . . . So it
is not gainsaid by the most rigid Anti-monarchists and wildest

6. E.g., ed. 1768, pp. 155ff.
7. *Brief Register*, Part I, Introduction [pp. 11, 14].
8. *Ibid.*, Part II, Introduction, 'To the Reader'. Prynne (1600–1669)
was the foremost controversialist of his day: perhaps he is best remembered
for his attack in 1632 on stage-plays, which was construed as reproving
the queen and cost him his ears in punishment.

Sectaries. Nevertheless, such hath been the Art and Industry of those common Disturbers of our Peace (as we plainly see) that they have, publicly as well as clandestinely, made it their endeavour to persuade the World that the Supreme Power and absolute Sovereignty doth totally reside in the People, and consequently in the Knights of the Shire, Citizens and burgesses of the Cities and Burroughs of this Realm as their Representatives. . . . By which Argument for fixing the Supreme Power in the People, the King is to be no other, in effect, than a Ministerial Officer to a Multitude and to give an Accompt to that confused Rout, when as often as they shall require it.' [9]

Of other controversialists of the time, we need refer only to William Petyt and Robert Brady, both men of extensive learning, whose voluminous works can still be read with profit, and both men, like Prynne, Keepers of the Records in the Tower. They too concentrated upon the composition of parliament and, within it, upon the commons and the part they played in politics. Brady, the stout supporter of monarchy, was opposed to 'such as hold forth to the People Ancient Rights and Privileges, which they have found out in Records and Histories, in Charters and other Monuments of Antiquity', and accordingly he wrote 'for the defence of Truth, and the Detection of these Men, and for no other purpose, and of their partial Citations, Falsity in leaving out and adding what they please, Mis-Applications, false Interpretations, wilful Wresting and abusing of Records and History'.[10] Of the men whom Brady set himself to controvert, Petyt was the best equipped. How this champion of parliament approached his subject in his desire to refute 'the absurd and malicious ignorance and fallacies of late writers' is amply shown in the title of his main book: *The Ancient Right of the Commons of England Asserted; or, A Discourse, Proving by Records and the Best Historians, that the Commons of England Were Ever an Essential Part of Parliament*.[11] Brady was by far the better scholar, but it was Petyt's views that won the day, even though he saw no

9. This quotation is from Dugdale's Preface.
10. From the Preface to *An Introduction to the Old English History* (1684).
11. Published in 1680.

difficulty in believing that the commons were, perhaps under the ancient Britons and certainly under the Saxons, an essential part of parliament.[12]

By a strange fatality, works written from a more detached historical standpoint remained in manuscript. Matthew Hale's *Jurisdiction of the Lords House of Parliament*, a remarkably able book, still too much ignored, was not published until 1796, a hundred and twenty years after his death. Thomas Madox, who had written a chapter on parliament for inclusion in his *History of the Exchequer* (1711), excluded it from that book because he had it in mind to write a separate work on parliament, and that work he did not live to achieve.[13] Hale's material was that common to parliamentary historians of the seventeenth century and he had a practical purpose in view of reforming the House of Lords. Madox was more original in that he drew his material from the records of the exchequer. He sought to keep his compilation of evidence free from 'establishing of any private opinions preconceived in my own mind', and his work would perhaps have been more likely to lead to a fresh consideration of the problems presented by the early history of parliament. But in any case the current conceptions of the seventeenth century had received a long start.

Nor was it only the scope of the evidence that was settled beforehand. The main conclusions in the *Lords Reports on the Dignity of a Peer* in the third decade of the nineteenth century were also decided for them by the antiquaries and controversialists of the seventeenth century. These *Reports* in their turn

12. For a convenient symposium of papers by leading antiquarians and scholars of the very early seventeenth century, see Thomas Hearne, *Collection of Curious Discourses*, i.281–310.

13. The excluded matter is to be found in British Museum, Additional MS. 4492. There are some jottings on the subject in Add. MS. 4491. It has now been printed by Miss Catherine S. Sims, 'An Unpublished Fragment of Madox, *History of the Exchequer*', in *Huntington Library Quarterly*, xxiii (1959), 61–94. Cf. p. 82: 'it seemeth that many cases, as well unsolemn as solemn, and many of small as of great weight, were transmitted from the king's other courts to his parliament or council. On the other part, sometimes pleas and other business were sent from the parliament or council to the exchequer (or some other of the king's courts) that justice might be done there.' It will be observed that Madox is studying the functions, not the composition, of parliament and is reading administrative records, not writs of summons.

determined the teaching of Stubbs, who relied upon them far more than is generally recognised. He in his turn became responsible for what, until some fifty years ago, was the universally accepted outline of the early history of parliament. There is no mistaking the chain of connexion.

The Lords Committees were not undertaking a dispassionate enquiry into the early history of parliament. Their view of it was settled by the object of their researches. The five volumes of their *Reports* are concerned with little else than what is termed 'the nature of the Legislative Assemblies of the country'.[14] It never occurred to their lordships to ask whether they were, in fact, dealing with a legislative assembly: they simply assumed that parliament must have been in the past what it had become in the present. Their efforts to find resemblances between, as they put it, 'the constituent parts of the Saxon Legislative Assemblies before the Conquest'[15] and the parliaments of Simon de Montfort and Edward I were thwarted, but what they could do they did, and they laid their emphasis upon popular representation, legislation, and taxation. This view of the medieval parliament is common to the *Lords Reports* and to the *Constitutional History* of Stubbs.[16] When Stubbs was writing, men were still looking for the origin of democratic institutions at a very early date. By his training Stubbs had a reverence for facts, but his inferences were not decided by the facts but by his inherited assumptions which arranged the facts in the traditional moulds. He committed the common fault, so frequently seen in historical documentaries on television, of reading history backwards and, instead of drawing his conclusions from the evidence, he imposed his conclusions on the evidence. It was inevitable that time and time again he was aware that many facts would not square with his assumptions and, because he was an honest worker, he recorded them. This is why it is often ingenuously thought

14. *Lords Reports*, i.4.
15. *Ibid.*, i.17.
16. Stubbs, *Select Charters* (9th ed.), p. 39: Parliament under Edward I 'implies . . . the existence of a national assembly, the representation in that assembly of all classes of freemen regularly summoned . . . and definite powers of taxation, legislation and general political deliberation'.

that the 'perfect hedger'—the phrase is not ours but Miss Cam's [17]—anticipated the arguments that were to flout his own. But it is surely naïve to continue to regard this as an indication of impartiality, for if impartiality means anything, it must mean that all the facts have been considered and carefully weighed and given an opportunity to influence the judgement.

The Lords Committees did not doubt that popular representatives formed an essential constituent element in parliament which was, by definition, an assembly of the 'three estates'. Stubbs saw no reason to differ. Yet early evidence indisputably showed that most parliaments, so termed by contemporaries, had no popular representatives present in them. Since *ex hypothesi* this could not be, therefore the Lords Committees came to the conclusion that the parliaments of Edward I were of two different kinds: 'assemblies regularly meeting at stated intervals and acting generally as the king's ordinary council or as a court of justice' and 'the Legislative Assemblies of the country'.[18] This dichotomy had quite escaped the notice of contemporary chroniclers and contemporary civil servants. Nevertheless Stubbs adopted the teaching of the Lords Committees and, it must be added, went on to darken their counsel. For whereas to the Lords Committees the judicial sessions were 'ordinary parliaments' and the sessions of the 'three estates' were 'extraordinary assemblies',[19] Stubbs chose to reverse the order: to him it was the judicial sessions that were 'special parliaments',[20] and he was clearly reluctant to apply the term 'parliament' to them at all, and at one time he incautiously excluded the dispensation of justice from the functions of parliament, asserting that 'the judicial power has never been exercised by the parliament as a parliament'.[21] And just as the Lords Committees saw in 1295 the great dividing line,

17. H. M. Cam, 'Stubbs Seventy Years After', *Cambridge Hist. Journal*, ix (1948), 143.
18. *Lords Reports on the Dignity of a Peer*, i.169.
19. *Ibid.*, pp. 170, 179, 180, 211.
20. *Constitutional History*, ii (1887 ed.), 274.
21. *Select Charters*, 1st ed. (1870), p. 45; 9th ed. (1913), p. 50. Cf. Sir Goronwy Edwards, *Historians and the Medieval English Parliament*, pp. 14f.: 'that judicial functions were performed in parliament . . . has never been denied'.

so also did Stubbs. The concept of the duality of parliaments has long persisted in other forms. It will even be found in Pollard's *Evolution of Parliament,* published in 1920, and it was not challenged by any reviewers of that book. He suggested that the chroniclers used the word 'parliament' to indicate a representative assembly and that the royal clerks reserved the term for a meeting of the king's council. The two bodies were summoned by different mandates, met at different times, and discharged different functions.[22] The slight evidence put forward in support of this literary phenomenon has not survived criticism.[23]

From the 1870s onwards Stubbs's views—and the views of others which were indistinguishable from his own—passed for a long while unchallenged. There was one solitary exception. The incomparable F. W. Maitland expressed serious doubts in some passages of his introduction to certain parliament rolls of 1305, which were published in 1893 in the Rolls Series under the short title of *Memoranda de Parliamento.* Maitland approached his documents as contemporary records which should be illustrated by other contemporary records. Here at last was the great break-through: the search for truth which was to be approached without suppositions, the refusal to be content to stand *super antiquas vias,* the determination to test the evidence anew and follow wherever it led, to furnish reasoned judgement instead of a rationalisation of preconceptions. He indicated, plainly enough, his difficulty in accepting current teaching; he suggested that others had looked at the thirteenth century 'through the distorting medium of the fourteenth' and that there had been much explaining away, as irregular and anomalous, of matters which merely conflicted with modern belief of what ought to have happened.[24] Maitland, of course, did more than this. He set himself to explain how one particular parliament did its work, how it was divided up into tribunals and committees, and who composed them. And he found that he had very little left for the 'commoners' (as he called them) to do. 'The king', he said, 'so far as we know, did

22. *Evolution of Parliament,* p. 51.
23. H. G. Richardson and G. O. Sayles, 'The Early Records of the English Parliament', *Bull. Inst. Hist. Research,* v (1928), 143–44.
24. Introduction, p. lxxxix.

not ask them for money, nor did he desire their consent to any new law'. What they did during their three weeks at Westminster was 'guesswork'.[25] When he declared that the king's council was the 'core of parliament', it was because he was interested in the functions of parliament, and previous writers like Elsynge and Madox, who had studied the records, had in this respect anticipated his argument. Maitland was well aware that his conclusions destroyed the traditional belief in 'an assembly of estates' as expressed in 'books that are already classical'. He was not, of course, referring to the *Lords Reports*, published three-quarters of a century earlier,[26] which were dull, unreadable, and unread, left like all such government-commissioned works to gather dust upon the shelves. He had in mind Stubbs's *Constitutional History*, which had at the time passed through many editions, and he tried to soften the blow, as he was to do half a dozen years later when he was compelled flatly to contradict Stubbs's teachings upon the attitude of the Church in England to canon law,[27] by impishly implying that his views did not seriously disturb current doctrine.

The legend of parliament was, indeed, too strongly entrenched. Maitland's introduction to the *Memoranda de Parliamento* did not attract a great deal of attention at the time of its publication. It was not thought important enough to be included, after his death, in his *Collected Essays*, it did not give rise immediately to doubts about current teaching, to the criticism of received doctrine, that it seems to us, nowadays, it should have done. It was not until the publication, in 1910, of C. H. McIlwain's essay *The High Court of Parliament and Its Supremacy* and, in 1920, of A. F. Pollard's *Evolution of Parliament* that there were signs that the leaven was working at last, both in America and in England. Neither of these books was the work of a professed medievalist, nor did either attempt a detailed account of medieval parliamentary institutions. But they were a challenge to medievalists to re-examine the early history of parliament.

And yet the challenge, so it seems, has been evaded by half-hearted compromises. However much the traditional story has

25. P. lxxv.
26. This is the opinion of Edwards, *op. cit.*, p. 10.
27. Cf. C. S. Fifoot, *Letters of Maitland*, no. 225.

been questioned in this field or that, the questioning has not seriously disturbed historians who believe that, by patching here and there, they can still produce a garment suited to modern needs. It may well be that myths have to be invented in order to explain, colour, and justify political and social change and, by so doing, provide a vision of the future rather than a view of the past. As a reflexion of public opinion they must, of course, be studied, but in their own right and not as portraying historical fact.

A few illustrations of current thought and teaching reveal the fetters forged so long ago. One recent method of examining the nature of parliament under Henry III has been to exclude the evidence of legal and financial records on the ground that they 'would necessarily yield a heavy predominance of specialised uses of the term'.[28] We must regret that it should be openly declared that evidence, acknowledged to be available, has not been permitted to inform the judgement. For the tendentious selection of facts is sadly reminiscent of Stubbs and, indeed, it would ignore the first known official use of the word 'parliament', found as it is upon a plea roll of 1236 so soon after the changes in the legal and administrative structure of government in 1234.[29] Again, the apparently ineradicable desire to emphasise the composition rather than the functions of parliament causes writs of summons to be placed in the forefront of the argument. Yet this ignores the undeniable fact that for the great majority of the parliaments of Henry III and Edward I no such writs are recorded. Where writs are issued, it is because parliament is to meet in an unusual place or because the business to be dealt with is out of the ordinary, making it particularly desirable to make sure that the council in parliament was adequately afforced, and they testify to what was exceptional and not to the norm. And even then the enrolment of such writs was selective, left, as is apparently al-

28. R. F. Treharne, 'The Nature of Parliament in the Reign of Henry III', *English Hist. Review*, lxxiv (1959), 593. The statement that the word 'parliament' disappears for two years after the battle of Evesham in 1265 is manifestly incorrect: even in the chancery rolls alone there is ample evidence for the parliament at Winchester in September 1265 and the parliament at Kenilworth in August 1266.

29. H. G. Richardson and G. O. Sayles, 'The Earliest Known Official Use of the Term "Parliament"', *English Hist. Review*, lxxxii (1967), 747-50.

ways the way with all chancery enrolments, to the caprice of
the enrolling clerks. Indeed, to treat recorded writs of summons as a truly representative sample exhibiting the nature of
parliament and the business ordinarily transacted in parliament
mirrors an approach inherited from the past. Most curious of
all is the statement that even under Edward III assemblies, var-
iously described as *parliamentum, tractatus, colloquium, consilium,* could not be distinguished.[30] We are asked to believe
that, when the barons in 1258 decided that each year three
parliaments would be held, they had no idea of what they
meant by parliament; and that when under Edward I men
are continually being ordered *tout court* to appear 'at the next
parliament', they did not know when or where to go. Let us
give a present-day analogy from the use of the simple word
'assembly'. If a member of the Presbyterian Church of Scotland informed a fellow-member that he would see him at the
Assembly, his friend did not require further information: he
knew that they would meet in Edinburgh and in the third
week of May, for the General Assembly of that Church is always
held there and then. A general word has been used with a
technical meaning but the context leaves no room for doubt.
So it was with parliament. Many years ago carefully constructed
tables, showing the incidence of English parliaments in the first
hundred and twenty years of their existence by scrupulous and
precise reference to official documents in particular, appeared
originally under the aegis of A. F. Pollard and were reproduced,
in abstract, in the first edition of the *Handbook of British
Chronology,* published in 1939.[31] The value of these tables
was obscured in the second revised edition of that handbook
in 1961 when parliaments were shuffled among a heterogeneous
collection of non-parliamentary assemblies, even meetings of a
few councillors to carry out the routine duties of the day.[32]
So devised, the list permits the entry of assemblies attended

30. M. McKisack, *The Fourteenth Century,* p. 182.
31. H. G. Richardson in *Trans. Royal Hist. Soc.,* 4th series, xi
(1928), 172–75; H. G. Richardson and G. O. Sayles in *Bull. Inst. Hist.
Research* v (1928), 151–54, vi (1928), 85–88, viii (1930), 78–82;
whence *Handbook,* pp. 342ff.
32. On such a basis the list could be extended indefinitely: e.g.,
King's Bench Roll, no. 301 (Trinity 1335), m. 48: councils at Westminster, Woodstock, and Osney in 1332–33.

by popular representatives—knights alone, burgesses alone, or merchants alone—which could find no possible place in a list of parliaments. Nothing more clearly reveals the desire to keep the history of parliament associated willy-nilly with the history of popular representation, with which for nearly a hundred years it had only an occasional connexion. Since the casual nature of this connexion can no longer be denied, an effort has been made to minimise its logical implications by drawing a distinction between 'pre-representative parliaments' and 'representative parliaments' as though 'representation' was the all-important consideration at the time.[33] Contemporaries did not think in these terms in the thirteenth century and they showed not the slightest interest in the fact that popular representatives had been summoned to meet the king in parliament instead of elsewhere. And when we recall that none were summoned to the parliament of 1310, which altered radically the way in which the country was governed, or to the parliament of Midsummer 1325, it is clear that 'pre-representative parliaments' are still being summoned after 'representative parliaments' had met, and the re-introduction of the notion of a duality of parliaments only helps to keep the representation of the people in the prominence in which it had been placed by the political controversialists of nearly four centuries ago. A study by a scholar in the United States of parliamentary literature in the seventeenth and eighteenth centuries evoked the cry that we 'should sharply limit our use of words like democracy, representative, the people'.[34] How much more pertinent these words are for the Middle Ages!

The traditional view of the medieval parliament has been given a further lease of life by the foundation of the History of Parliament Trust in 1951, endowed by the British Government with £340,000 to be spent over a period of twenty years. As we would expect, despite the name of the Trust, it is not the history of parliament that is to be studied but the history of simply the House of Commons. Certainly for the period be-

33. Edwards, *op. cit.*, pp. 8–24.
34. Caroline Robbins, 'Why the English Parliament Survived the Age of Absolutism', in *Studies Presented to the International Commission for the History of Representative and Parliamentary Institutions* (Louvain, 1958), p. 205.

fore the Reformation Parliament of 1529, which marks the most reasonable dividing line between parliament as a medieval and as a modern institution, the scheme is founded on false assumptions and wrong priorities. We only delude ourselves if we believe that an understanding of the medieval parliament can be reached by compiling biographies of members of the House of Commons. The simple fact that nearly sixty of the first seventy parliaments from 1258 were not attended by any popular representatives makes nonsense of the initial approach to the subject. And the dynamic history of an institution cannot be learned from the biographies of its members. No one would pretend to understand today the part played by the Church of England in national life by reading the pages of Crockford [35] or the part played by parliament by perusing *Dods Parliamentary Companion*.[36] To still pretend that the history of the medieval parliament is being written when the sparse and uninformative details of the obscure lives of obscure men are laboriously collected because they made a fitful appearance among the commons is merely to veil the hard realities of medieval politics in what was an essentially aristocratic society. The way in which such institutions do their business—their functions, their procedures, their committees, the extent of their powers, and the restraints upon those powers—these are the vital matters and they are not disclosed by biographical information. Such has its place, of course, and a study of some, but not all, parliamentarians may be necessary for an understanding of the institution they served, but the place of biography in constitutional history is a subordinate one. And it is to be feared that the History of Parliament Trust bolsters up the popular but erroneous belief that the commons did not so much co-operate in government, which was the sole purpose of their summons, as spend their time in opposing the king as the executive. If we see in parliament merely a public spectacle of political struggles between Crown and Commons and of democracy in embryo, we shall certainly never understand the medieval parliament. For agreement, not dispute, was the aim

35. *Crockford's Clerical Directory* (London). This gives each year the names, education, careers, and benefices of the Anglican clergy.
36. *Dods Parliamentary Companion* (London).

and object of it all and the commons had a duty to support the government, though, like the lords, they on occasion resisted it. When we consider priorities, what we need above all else—and it is so obvious that it seems otiose to state it—is the publication of the records of parliament: not only of the parliament rolls in a modern edition, based at long last on the originals themselves,[37] but of related documents, drawn from plea rolls, exchequer memoranda, chancery enrolments and miscellanea, the files of petitions, the ancient correspondence, thus reconstructing the administrative machine which culminated with the king in council in his parliaments.[38] It is surely remarkable that the country which prides itself on being the mother of parliaments should not bother to make the early records of its own parliament available. There will, however, be little to tell what exactly the commons did in parliament. If they were highly important, we have a right to expect such importance to be revealed by documents, and it is somewhat ironic that for a knowledge of the activities of the Lower House we must go to the records of the Upper House and read there of the occasional conferences where representatives of the lords at the request of the commons agreed to meet their representatives in order to assist them in their deliberations.[39] Let us at least remember that in the fifteenth century Francesco dei Coppini, the papal legate who witnessed the overthrow of Henry VI in 1460 and played some part in that episode,[40] described the English parliament to the pope as an assembly of prelates and nobles and disregarded the commons

37. For example, if the medieval clerks marked passages they had written for deletion, the transcribers dutifully ignored the instructions, no matter how instructive the omissions are to the historian. And no one, reading the printed version in *Rot. Parl.*, ii. 303–60 of Parliament Rolls, nos. 27–30, could possibly be aware that they include the actual rolls of common petitions as they came before the council, on which the council's answers have been inserted on the spot in different ink.

38. T. F. T. Plucknett's statement that parliament rolls and petitions 'form the sum of our parliamentary records' (*English Government at Work*, i. 93) is in its implications misleading.

39. Out of thirty-four parliaments, meeting between 1373 and 1407, only ten are known to have such conferences, nearly all belonging to the years 1373–84 and the reign of Henry IV (K. B. McFarlane in *Trans. Royal Hist. Soc.*, 4th series, xxvi, [1944], 54, n.1).

40. J. H. Ramsay, *Lancaster and York*, ii. 223f.

entirely.[41] We cannot write off this calculating Italian as a poor,
ignorant foreigner. In his considered opinion, in the high politics of the England he knew, the commons did not count. To
him the forefront of the stage was occupied by a few men,
whose biographies have long been written in the *Complete
Peerage* [42] or the *Dictionary of National Biography*,[43] and he
paid no attention to the back of the stage where the commons
stood crowded together.[44]

This then is the lesson we would teach. The king's parliaments were at all times of one kind only. The story is of a court,
a court set above all other courts and departments of government. It was for the king to decide whether or not the assembly he had in mind should be a parliament or not; it was
for him to decide whether legislation should be passed or
taxation discussed or popular representatives summoned. The
traditional conception of the medieval parliament must be rejected and with it must depart the belief that the parliament
of the thirteenth century in England was *sui generis*, a unique
phenomenon. For it falls into line with what was happening
elsewhere in Western Europe and only thereby does its history
become intelligible to us. The fourteenth century will witness
divergencies from continental developments but they will be
far from producing a 'democratic' institution. Perhaps, in an
old-fashioned way, we may end with a moral. In history we
must make sure that, if the evidence does not square with our
hypothesis, we discard the hypothesis and do not prefer instead
to explain away the facts. As T. H. Huxley put it long ago, it
is always sad to slay a beautiful hypothesis with hard facts, but
it is preferable to sitting like hens on hard-boiled eggs.

41. *Commentaries of Pius II*, Book III (trans. in Smith College
Studies in History, xxv (1939–40), 270): 'The prelates and nobles of
the realm (parliament as they called it) convened in London to discuss
matters of state'.
42. *Complete Peerage*, ed. Vicary Gibb (London, 1910–59).
43. Published in 1885–1901, republished in 1908–9.
44. Cf. A. F. Pollard in *English Hist. Review*, lvii (1942), 40, n.3:
'During the early part of the sixteenth century parliament was used of the
lords without reference to the commons'.

2. Commune Consilium
and Parliamentum

We must explain, as well as the limited sources at
our disposal permit, the place in the administration occupied
by the body whose right and duty it was to advise and, according to one view, to control the king—the baronage. Three terms
will fall to be discussed in this connexion: *commune consilium,
colloquium* and *parliamentum.* While our main concern lies
with the evolution of administrative processes under Henry
III, we have deemed it desirable to introduce some earlier history in order that the exposition may be reasonably clear and
complete.

The king always had his court around him, his household
officers, the clerks of his chapel, a few dignitaries, ecclesiastical
or secular, in attendance. But there were times when he needed
weightier counsel than these could give. There may have been
occasions when a special summons was sent to assemble the
great men of the realm, but a regular opportunity was afforded
for consulting them, irrespective of summons, in the gatherings
at the three great feasts of the year, Christmas, Easter, and,
seven weeks later, Whitsunday. Then the king wore his cere-
monial crown; a votive mass was celebrated; chants (*laudes*)
were sung in his honour; there were feastings at which the
titular officers of the royal household performed their honorific
duties. It would have been an affront to the king for any magnate without good excuse to absent himself. This custom was
established in England at least as early as the tenth century

and quite possibly two centuries earlier, for these crown-wearings or *coronationes* were the sequel to the ceremony of conse-
crating and anointing the king at the beginning of his reign,
at his 'ordination', as it was then called, and this ceremony
(which we term coronation) was known in England in the
eighth century at much the same time as it was in France.[1]
So when the Norman kings adopted the practice of coronation
and crown-wearing, they were following the custom of English
kings and were not importing an outlandish fashion from beyond the Channel.

Now, while we know in a general way what happened on
the occasion of a solemn crown-wearing, we rarely have any
details of the happenings on any particular occasion. The evidence of charters suggests that a good deal of business was
reserved for the great feasts and we know, for example, that
the Christmas crown-wearing in the last year of his life was
chosen by Edward the Confessor for the dedication of his
great church at Westminster. A more appropriate occasion
might seem to have been one of the feasts of St. Peter, to
whom the church was dedicated; but Christmas was chosen
because there would be assembled at Westminster a great con-
course of prelates and nobles. To monastic annalists such an
event as the dedication of a great church was more notable
than political events, except those of a catastrophic kind, and
even the twelfth-century chronicler, Roger of Howden, who
was interested in politics and administration, rarely informs
us of the business transacted at the great festivals. He tells us,
quite exceptionally, that in 1170 the king kept the Easter feast
at Windsor and then moved on to London to hold a 'great
council' where the coronation of his eldest son was discussed,
the laws (*statuta regni*) were reviewed, and widespread changes
in the subordinate administration were made by removing most
of the existing sheriffs and their bailiffs.[2] But Howden has
nothing definite to say of the council at Clarendon that met
in the winter of 1165–66, presumably in connexion with the
Christmas festivities, where some momentous legislation was
promulgated. It is only by inference that we can be reasonably

1. Richardson and Sayles, *Governance of Mediaeval England*, pp.
397–412.
2. *Gesta Regis Henrici Secundi*, i.4–5.

sure that on this occasion extensive innovations were made in the criminal law, in the land law, and in the organisation of judicial eyres.[3]

If, however, we have a little flickering light to illuminate the assemblies of magnates at the great feasts before the Norman Conquest and during the centuries before the reign of Henry III, hardly any light at all is cast upon assemblies that met on other occasions. We can be certain that any such assemblies outside the regular cycle would be altogether exceptional, for it would be unreasonable to expect earls and barons to leave their estates with any frequency, bishops to leave their dioceses, abbots to leave their monasteries. There were, of course, court-bishops and there were some earls and barons who stayed for considerable periods in the king's company; but we are speaking of the rank and file. The lay magnates would be called, too often for the liking of most of them, to follow the king in his wars. They had no wish to make unprofitable journeys to court, and, if needs must, they wanted long notice. We have, of course, the famous chapter in Magna Carta providing for a forty-day summons of the magnates, but only for the purpose of obtaining their reluctant consent to an unusual aid or to scutage,[4] matters which, it seems evident, would not normally be expected to be broached at one of the great feasts. This requirement of a forty-day summons was dropped from re-issues of the Charter, but since a period of forty days re-appears as the minimum length of summons in parliamentary writs, we seem justified in believing that it had been usually observed under Henry III when extraordinary great councils were summoned. The few writs of summons that have survived from the reign of John do not, however, suggest that he had been showing equal consideration. Exact compliance could hardly have been expected to a writ, despatched to the bishops towards the end of April 1205, not only requiring them to be present at a council in London on 15 May, but directing them to summon the abbots and priors of the religious houses within their dioceses to be present also. And a writ to the sheriffs dated 7 November 1213, requiring them

3. Richardson and Sayles, *op. cit.*, pp. 197–200, 439–44; *Law and Legislation*, pp. 93–96.
4. Magna Carta, c. 14.

to send four knights to a council at Oxford on the fifteenth, seems merely derisory.[5] We can but wonder whose folly inspired such an absurdity.

The convenience of making use of the assemblies at the principal feasts for holding great councils gradually disappeared. Clearly Henry II's numerous and prolonged absences meant that the ceremony of crown-wearing had become relatively infrequent in England, while under Richard I it must have been practically unknown. The only occasion of which we have knowledge is when at Easter 1194 a crown-wearing provided the means of rehabilitating Richard after his captivity.[6] But under John regular crown-wearings were resumed and Henry III found them so much to his liking that their number increased until in one year they amounted to sixteen.[7] This multiplicity, while it gratified the childish vanity of the king, deprived the occasion of any other significance. Magnates and prelates might with some reluctance attend three festivities at court in the year, but not sixteen. Those living at any distance from the court would have had little time spared them for their own affairs, had they graced all these occasions for the exaltation of the king's majesty. It will be clear, when we come to discuss the Provisions of Oxford, that three attendances at afforced meetings of the council were as much as could be expected from most magnates, and experience was to show that many were not prepared to attend so frequently. We must not imagine that there was any eagerness on the part of prelates or barons to counsel, much less to control, the king. Only in desperate crises would they seek to do so. At other times it was the king, faced, as he was, with the necessity of consulting the magnates, who sought their counsel, or at least their acquiescence, in major decisions of policy or in important judgements of the king's court.

Though we lack detailed knowledge of the practice in the twelfth century, the accepted doctrine is set out in the *Leges Edwardi Confessoris* near the beginning of Henry II's reign and

5. *Rot. Litt. Claus.*, i.28–29, 33, 165. Both these writs are reprinted in Stubbs, *Select Charters* (9th ed., pp. 277, 282) from the *Lords Reports on the Dignity of a Peer*. Stubbs did not notice the difficulties involved.

6. Roger of Howden, *Chronica*, iii.248.

7. E. H. Kantorowicz, *Laudes Regiae*, pp. 175–76.

in the lawbook that goes under the name of Glanville at its close.[8] Both stress the necessity under which the king lies of acting with the advice of his barons. Much earlier the doctrine is implied, if it is not explicitly stated, in Henry I's coronation charter, that changes in the law are only to be made with the counsel of the barons.[9] When, from the reign of John, records begin to accumulate, we find that practice accords with doctrine. The chancery clerks seem to be careful to record that major decisions are taken by 'common counsel' of the barons.

The Middle Ages knew of no such body as the Common Council (*commune concilium*) though it finds a place of importance in Stubbs's teaching and in many derivative books, even surprisingly in some recent ones.[10] Better spelled *commune consilium*, the phrase means 'general' or 'unanimous' advice—like our modern 'common consent'—doubtless a formal unanimity but, after all, the preamble of a modern statute still ignores the dissent of any minority. Sometimes this advice tended to become personified, and then the phrase was so used as seemingly to cover both the advice and the advisers. In much the same way the word *parliamentum* referred to an event and came to mean a body of persons engaged in a certain function.[11] Yet *commune consilium* never had the good fortune to be applied as a technical term for a major administrative or political body and never meant, as the older constitutional historians imagined, an assembly of magnates that developed into parliament or became known as a parliament.[12] It is, however, the use of the phrase in connexion with an assembly of magnates that interests us here.

The full phrase is 'by the common counsel of our barons' (*communi consilio baronum nostrorum*) or, as Bracton put it, echoing the phraseology of chapters 12 and 14 of the Great

8. Richardson and Sayles, *Law and Legislation*, pp. 57f.; *Glanvill* (ed. G. D. G. Hall), Prologue, p. 2.

9. C. 13; cf. c. 1 (Liebermann, *Gesetze*, i.521–22).

10. For instance, J. E. A. Jolliffe, *Constitutional History of Medieval England* (ed. 1954): the references are conveniently collected in the index.

11. Note, however, the very early personification of parliament in February 1248: 'it was adjudged in our court before us and all our parliament' (*Close Rolls*, 1247–51, p. 107).

12. The older doctrine could not survive the acute analysis by the American scholar, A. B. White, 'Was There a "Common Council" before Parliament?', *American Hist. Review*, xxv (1919), 1–17.

Charter of 1215, 'by the counsel of the whole realm' (*consilio totius regni*): [13] we put the phrase in the ablative case because it is but rarely found in any other form. This, of itself, should suggest that we have to deal not with a "common council' of barons but with the advice they offer, whether about the assize of bread at Easter 1204, or the distribution of the king's galleys among various ports, or the decision that every nine knights should provide a tenth knight for the king's service,[14] or the surrender of the kingdom to the pope.[15]

When we proceed to the reign of Henry III we find closely similar phraseology employed to express the concurrence of the magnates, whether to the ordinance for the conservation of the peace on 1 June 1233 or to the arrest of armed men on the highways or a veto on tournaments.[16]

The year 1233 is a convenient one at which to pause in our consideration of the reciprocal duty of the barons to give counsel and the king to receive it, for the following year was to bring great changes, whose causes and consequences will be traced later. We turn therefore to discuss that other function of the barons, their participation in important judgements of the king's court, a duty that fell upon lay magnates and ecclesiastical magnates alike. The Constitutions of Clarendon of 1164, regulating the relations between Church and State, had stated quite explicitly that, in the king's view, archbishops and bishops, like everybody else who held a barony of the king, were under the duty of taking part in the judgements of his court, being excused only in cases involving death or mutilation.[17] Here we have a principle that is of great importance in the evolution of parliament and one we must bear in mind when we come to consider the development of petitory procedure: barons, lay and eccclesiastical—one day men will call them peers—are judges in the king's court.

So far as the ordinary courts were concerned, though for a time bishops and abbots continue to be found sitting in the central courts or acting as justices in eyre, their employment

13. Bracton, *De Legibus*, fol. 413*b*.
14. *Rot Litt. Pat.*, pp. 41, 52*b*, 55.
15. *Foedera*, i.115.
16. *Close Rolls*, 1231–34, pp. 309–10, 317, 318.
17. Constitutions of Clarendon, c. xi.

in such a capacity inevitably dwindled with the growing tech-
nicality of English jurisprudence and the rise of the literate
layman and especially the professional lawyers; and the thirteenth century was to witness the gradual exclusion of ecclesiastical dignitaries from the courts of common law.[18] This with-
drawal from the courts was not, of course, peculiar to ecclesiastical dignitaries: the same causes that excluded them excluded
lay barons equally. They were, as a body, no longer profes-
sionally competent. This disqualification served, however,
rather to enhance their status: to continue in office would now
have been beneath their dignity. It required an extraordinary
situation, such as that following the parliament of Oxford of
1258, to induce barons, lay and ecclesiastical, to take an active
part in judicial work. We must not anticipate our later discussion: but we must point out the change in the status of the
baronage, a gradual change, liable to twists and turns, but
tending always in the same upward direction. It is, however,
the presence of the baronage in the highest of all courts that
concerns us now.

Let us take the story back as far as we reasonably can.
Until the reign of Henry I there was no organised, central
judicature in England.[19] The Norman Conquest of England in
1066 would not have had its momentous consequences but for
the English Conquest of Normandy in 1106. For by William
I's will England and Normandy were divided and parted company; the duchy going to his eldest son, Robert, the kingdom
to his second son, William Rufus. The two countries were intended to follow their own quite independent ways and this, in
fact, they did for twenty years, and it seemed likely that the
Normans in England would be absorbed by the English as their
fellow-Northmen had been before them. But in 1106 the Con-
queror's third son, then Henry I of England, made war upon
his brother Robert, wrested Normandy from him, and formed
the Anglo-Norman state that was to endure for the next hundred years. We do well to remind ourselves that the kings of
England were not Englishmen: they were Frenchmen, French

18. Richardson and Sayles, *Governance of Mediaeval England*, pp.
318–20.
19. *Ibid.*, pp. 173–90.

in their language, French in their culture, French in their interests. Henry I lived in Normandy for half his reign of thirty-five years; Henry II, the greatest of the medieval kings of England, spent only thirteen years in England out of the thirty-four years he reigned; Richard I gave only five months out of his ten years as king to living within his kingdom. Therefore England had to face a problem of government that had not risen in Western Europe since the fall of the Roman Empire so many hundreds of years before: the problem of government in absence, of ruling England when the king was in Normandy and of ruling Normandy when the king was in England. The answer was found in the creation in both countries during Henry I's reign of the court of the exchequer and the office of justiciar, the *alter ego* of the king, governing during the king's absence and, when the king was present, continuing to uphold the burden of administration. So the twelfth century was the 'Age of the Justiciars' from Roger of Salisbury to Ralph Glanville, Hubert Walter to Geoffrey fitz Peter, men who helped to devise that machinery of government which placed England administratively a hundred years ahead of Capetian France.

But when, with the institution of the justiciarship and the court of the exchequer, a corps of regularly employed judges was constituted, men could not fail to perceive a difference between a routine court and an afforced court over which, quite exceptionally, the king presided. Routine judicial administration was conducted by the justiciar, who, from the nature of his office, could rarely be absent from England, while the king —we pass over Stephen's reign—was but intermittently in England and, even so, was continually travelling, rarely staying anywhere for more than a few days. However, administration tended more and more to be concentrated in one place which, if it was once at Winchester, had, by the second half of the twelfth century, become normally fixed at Westminster.

In principle, when the king was present in the kingdom, the justiciar no longer had independent authority—he was, after all, but a delegate—and his court was subsumed in the court before the king (*coram rege*). In practice, however, the justiciar continued to bear the burden of administration and it was only on comparatively infrequent occasions that the king pre-

sided over sessions of his court. When he did so, he was
attended by magnates, by bishops and barons, but the judicial
establishment, if we may so term it, the justiciar and judges,
were present also. The magnates may add dignity to the court
and weight to its findings, but the presence of the permanent
judiciary indicates that there is but one tribunal, despite the
presence of the king and despite the varying personnel. The
court is the king's court, whether the king presides or the justiciar. But although there is only one court and one corps of
judges, these special occasions when there is a numerously attended court are obviously distinguishable from routine sessions, and, when the king presides, we should expect that the
cases before the court would then be of particular importance
or of special interest to the king. And this is what we find in
the sparse records that have come down to us. There is perhaps
some danger in arguing from such cases as are known to us,
for naturally enough unimportant cases would have small
chance of being recorded. But though the king is the fountain
of justice and is accessible to all men, it is hard to believe that
trivial matters would come at this time before specially afforced courts or that the magnates would be troubled with
trifles when they assembled at the great feasts. The instances of
sessions of the court before the king (*coram rege*) are not
numerous in the twelfth century [20] but they constitute a
continuous chain of evidence for the exercise of judicial functions by afforced courts. When we reach the reign of John we
are in a different climate. Not only are surviving records relatively copious and fairly continuous, but the judicature may
now be regarded as professional, legal procedure as systematised
and regular, the result of thirty years and more of steady
growth and progress. Furthermore, a king is now on the throne
who concerns himself more with the details of administration
than did the pococurantist Richard. For in 1204 King John had
lost Normandy, in the event irretrievably, and no longer had
anywhere convenient to go abroad. The loss of Normandy affected the whole future of England and changed entirely the
basis of administration. The king was to become a stay-at-home
monarch, the justiciarship an anachronism. In consequence, we
hear much more of afforced courts thereafter. We choose but

20. *Ibid.*, pp. 210–15.

two illustrations to throw light upon their composition and functions. John was hearing a dispute in July 1204 between William the Marshal and others concerning the ownership of the manor of Sturminster. Perhaps because the parties were important, the proceedings were held before the king himself. Since a decision on so complicated a matter was difficult, the king adjourned the case for a few days when judgement was to be given to the parties by counsel of the court. The king asked his counsellors for advice, but they protested that they were so few and the circumstances so unusual that it would be better to defer the whole matter until 16 August when the archbishop of Canterbury, Hubert Walter, and the other great and wise men of the land would be able to be present. Finally a day seems to have been given to the parties to appear on 19 August. Now, upon that day there was an important meeting at Worcester, which lasted several days, and to it came Llewelyn, prince of North Wales, and Madog ap Gruffydd under safe-conduct in the company of the Marshal and the earl of Salisbury.[21] No record of the adjourned hearing of the action over the manor of Sturminster appears to have survived, but that is a minor loss. What is important is that here we have an example of the conjuncture of political and judicial business at a session of an afforced court.

Our next example of judicial business before an afforced court we take from the reign of Henry III, during that king's minority when in consequence there could be no court *coram rege*. There is but one central court, which normally sits at Westminster and which is known as the 'great court'. The case with which we are concerned was heard at Easter 1219.[22] During the recent civil war the earl of Chester had taken Maurice de Gaunt prisoner at the battle of Lincoln in May 1217 and put him to ransom. To secure his liberty Maurice agreed to pay the earl 1,500 marks, together with five horses and five hawks: in default of payment the earl was to have two of Maurice's manors to be held at a nominal rent. The stipulated term having arrived and Maurice being unable to find the

21. *Curia Regis Rolls*, iii. 124, 147, *Rot. Litt. Pat.*, p. 44: discussed by H. G. Richardson in *Trans. Royal Hist. Soc.*, 4th series, xi (1928), 165f.
22. *Rolls of the Justices in Eyre for Yorkshire*, 1218–19, ed. D. M. Stenton, pp. 413–14.

money for his ransom, the earl came to Westminster and there
before the king's council and the magnates of the land he produced the written agreement and had it read. Maurice was
apparently present and, while he admitted that the agreement
had been made, he protested that this was under duress. The
court, however, awarded seisin of the manors to the earl. Not-
withstanding this judgement, Maurice brought an assize of
novel disseisin against the earl before the justices in eyre. In
the eyre court the earl's bailiff pleaded, in effect, that Maurice
was estopped by the judgement of the great court, and the
justices therefore adjourned the case for hearing there. The
court, which was again composed of the king's council and the
magnates, held that they were bound by their previous judgement. We observe that it was not exceptional to afforce the
court in this way when important people or particularly difficult
cases were concerned. And then we remark the language in
which the record speaks of court and council. Maurice, it says,
'came to the great court and there was a discussion before the
council of the lord king and before the magnates'. There is no
mention of the judges but we must understand them to be
included in the council, and in this context 'council' means a
small, mainly ministerial body, in attendance on the king. The
magnates come to afforce this council and apparently those
summoned are not the body of tenants in chief, but a select
few, who, before long, will be said to be "of the lord king's
council'.

We have discussed sufficiently for our immediate purpose
two of the functions of the baronage, to give their counsel to
the king and to assist his court in delivering judgement.
There remains a third function: their right to be consulted, and
their duty to assent, when the king proposes to levy a scutage
or to demand an aid. This aspect of afforced sessions of the
council has received great, and perhaps disproportionate, attention at the hands of historians, partly because of the provisions of chapter 12 of the Great Charter of 1215 and partly
because of the importance attached to taxation in the later history of parliament. But this chapter 12 was omitted when the
Charter was re-issued in 1216, and though limitations are
placed in later issues of the Charter on the rate at which
scutage should be levied, there is no further provision for con-

sultation with the baronage. Any such provision was, in fact, probably unnecessary, for it seems to have been customary, as it was certainly prudent, to discuss any extraordinary taxation in an afforced council. Scutage could not be regarded as an extraordinary tax, but such a tax as the Saladin Tithe of 1188 or those taxes for discharging Richard I's ransom were obviously extraordinary. Of any debate between the king's ministers and the barons on these occasions, we are told as little by the chroniclers as we are told of the nature of the summons to the council or the numbers of barons summoned. Such details were not matters of interest to them.

We cannot give as much light and colour to an account of the early history of afforced councils as we would desire. But it is important to know that already in the twelfth century there is an institution—to avoid ambiguity, let us call it rather a contrivance of government—whereby there is summoned to the king's court an assembly of barons, who may counsel the king on political or administrative issues, on taxation, on judgements to be rendered by his court. This assembly is not a court of itself; it is not an organ of government; it has no definite constitution. It is but an intermittent phase of the king's court. If men distinguish these assemblies at all, they may call them a 'great council'.[23] We can describe this anomalous institution, but we can hardly define it. By the 1230's, however, there are in train events that will give this amorphous body shape; and now for the first time, so far as our knowledge goes, the king's clerks began to apply to these assemblies the name of 'parliament'. Before we explain why they did so, for the explanation may help to clear away some misapprehensions which, in various ways, have distorted the history of the English constitution, let us say something upon the word 'parliament' itself.

The origin and early use of the word 'parliament' have

23. See Howden on the assembly of 1170 (above, p. 22). So also the assembly at Westminster in February 1237 (below, p. 40). Note also that, when the judge Martin Patshill wrote to the chancellor in or before 1229, he advised him to postpone sending judges in circuit 'at the present time and before the assembly and meeting of the magnates (*ante congregacionem et conventum magnatum*), which will be at London at Three Weeks after Michaelmas, because they can then provide many things for the welfare of the realm that are not yet provided' (Ancient Correspondence, vol. vi, no. 128).

been much discussed and need not long detain us.[24] The
important step in any enquiry into its meaning must be to
consider all the institutions that bore the name, for it would
seem evident that an institution which was known by the
Romance name of 'parliament' in England, Ireland, and Scotland, in France, Italy, and Spain must have everywhere some
like purpose, some common features.[25] Of course, every institution must obviously have regard to the administrative
peculiarities of the country in which it is found, but it would
seem improbable that a name so generally used should be applied at the start of things to very dissimilar contrivances. We
have but to compare the parliament rolls of England and of
Ireland under Edward I, of Scotland under John Balliol, of
Toulouse under Alfonse of Poitiers, of Paris under Philip the
Fair, to realise how much there was once in common between
all the parliaments of the French-speaking world. And when
'parliament', used from the end of the eleventh century to indicate a 'parley' (*parlement*) or treaty, came eventually to be
applied to solemn courts, it was a word that indicated a
procedure different from that of a formal court of law, it implied a discussion rather than a judgement. It slowly made its
way in England into formal and official documents, though for
a long time many clerks regarded it as a vulgar word, a layman's word, even after it had become latinised as *parliamentum*: it is a word that a fastidious stylist will avoid, for which
he will substitute in preference the classical *colloquium*. Nevertheless men became accustomed to the use of 'parliament' and
the word crept into records of the most respectable class. In
1234 we find it in the accounts of royal officers in France;
in 1236 it is seen in England on the plea rolls of the court
of king's bench, in 1242 on the close roll, in 1248 on the
memoranda rolls of the exchequer. In all these instances parliament means a special meeting of the king's court. Hence-

24. H. G. Richardson, *op. cit.*, xi. 137–49 and Antonio Marongiu,
Medieval Parliaments: A Comparative Study (1962; trans. 1968), pp. 48f.
    25. Were it not explicable by preconceptions, it would be a curiosity
of literature that, when Stubbs looked abroad for institutions comparable
with the English parliament, he saw only the Spanish Cortes, the German
Diets, the French Estates-general, even 'the Swedish Diet composed of
clergy, barons, burghers and peasants' (*Constitutional History*, iii.167),
i.e., assemblies of estates, and ignored the assemblies that styled themselves
parliaments.

forward it continues to appear, in that technical sense, in public records until in the Provisions of Oxford in 1258 it was given official recognition. By 1299 it was being argued in court that by the custom of England no parliament relating to the kingdom could take place without the king and his council.[26] This is to express in slightly different words the description of parliament given in the legal treatise called *Fleta* and written round about the same year: 'The king has his court in his council in his parliaments'.[27] It is true that the word 'parliament' did not cease from being used in varying senses, but this is true of so many words whose meaning is made perfectly clear by the context in which they occur.[28] In the context of politics and law the king's parliament had only one meaning: it is a court, it is an afforced council, it is the parliament of *Fleta*.

26. *Calendar of Early Mayors' Court Rolls*, p. 25.
27. *Fleta*, ed. H. G. Richardson and G. O. Sayles, ii.109.
28. In this respect it is no different from other words and phrases like 'the king's court' (*curia regis*), 'before the king' (*coram rege*), 'law', 'custom', which have several senses all at the same time.

3. The Emergence of the King's Parliament

When philosophers and political thinkers could in these years engage themselves in subtle arguments and lawyers were fashioning the common law of England in all its complexities, it is hard to believe that administrators—bishops and barons, ministers and judges—could not reach firm and clear-cut decisions upon problems of government which had been under discussion for many years. We do not hesitate to regard the year 1234 as a memorable one, not only because it saw the end of a major revolt against the capricious rule of Henry III, but because it saw a deliberate change in the structure of government. The two events are linked: as in 1258, the threat of rebellion had to precede reform.

The hard fact that the king no longer had any business in Normandy had for thirty years been diminishing the responsibility of the justiciar. However reluctant royal circles might be to recognise it, the office had lost its primary purpose and, as year after year went by and the hope of regaining Normandy became dimmer and dimmer, the utility of the justiciarship must have become questionable to all. And when Henry III took to disliking his principal minister, Hubert de Burgh, and found his control, and probably his prudence, increasingly irksome, and when he turned from him to the Poitevin, Peter des Roches, the end was in sight.

Furthermore, the loss of Normandy led to changed conceptions of domestic government. So long as the kings were largely absentee rulers and the office of justiciar had been a reality, the evolution of a royal council with an inner core of constant composition was hardly possible. It was only when the king was resident in England that the principal ministers could assemble round him without the constant interruptions caused by those protracted visits abroad that left some of them at home and took others overseas. So, when John was bereft of Normandy in 1204, he began to form a group of counsellors around him in England, not all of them frequently in attendance but to whom he was more likely to turn than to others. We begin to hear less of the *curia regis* and more of the *consilium regis*, the king's council, which emerged to take on responsibilities that had so long lain with the justiciars. It was to be mainly composed of the king's ministers and judges, though bishops and barons who happened to be at court might join it in its deliberations: it remained continuously in existence to deal day by day with routine administration, and upon it the machinery of government was to turn until well into the modern age, and it was, in particular, to form, in Maitland's phrase, the core of parliament.

The final parting of the ways, the discarding of old traditions of government and the adoption of newly devised methods, came, as we have said, in 1234 and it did not come, it should be noted, through the initiative of the king. Henry III was not an Englishman or a Norman but a Frenchman, sprung from Angevins and Poitevins. His mother had become remarried in 1220 to a noble in her native Poitou and Henry's blind devotion to his French half-brothers, the Lusignans, was notorious. Henry's sympathies were with men whom the English barons, French though they were in speech, looked upon with aversion and dislike as aliens. Furthermore, the king was believed to be implicated in the plot in 1234 to murder Richard, the Earl Marshal, who had headed a group of barons in opposition and been driven into open revolt against him.[1] At a great council at Gloucester in mid-May 1234 Henry, the object of censure, disgust, and anger, bowed to the storm and,

1. Only the chronicler Roger of Wendover gives the detailed account of how Henry sealed the letters ordering the taking of the Earl Marshal alive or dead, and we must always be sceptical of his stories. At all events, the rumour, true or false, was believed (*Flores*, iv.292–93, 311).

reluctantly and grudgingly, dismissed his minster, Peter des Roches, and his associates, as well as Stephen Segrave, the last justiciar of the old line and a mere shadow of what justiciars had been in the past. The sentences of outlawry, passed irregularly upon Hubert de Burgh and others, were formally and publicly reversed: this reversal is notable because the king's own acts were under review, for it had been at his instance and not by due process of law that the sentences had been pronounced. Whoever added comments to the text of Henry Bracton, the judge who wrote a long and authoritative treatise on the common law, may have had this act of the council of Gloucester in mind when he said that the king was under the law and that, if in his conduct he was unbridled, it was the duty of his court to restrain him.[2] And during these momentous days from 16 May to 4 June there was discussed the re-organisation of the administration, which was evidently carried through piecemeal. The changes in the structure of government in 1234 are not likely to have been the chance result of a palace revolution. The storm had been impending for many months, and nobles and prelates, as well as royal ministers, were not caught unawares. Certainly the reform of the judicature had a great deal of thought behind it. And the changes in great councils and parliaments were in 1234, as they were to be in 1258, induced by the threat of armed conflict, and in neither instance could the king be certain that he would emerge victorious.

Since the justiciarship had become meaningless, it could be suppressed without loss[3] and henceforward the office was to remain unfilled. Three courts of common law were organised: the king's bench, the common bench, and the exchequer, and additional judges and barons of the exchequer were appointed. Men may have been thinking on these lines for some years. In the Great Charter of 1215 the barons had insisted that common pleas (that is, actions between private litigants) should be tried in a specified place, normally Westminster. They had no thought of restricting in any way actions in which the king was interested or of depriving aggrieved parties of their

2. Bracton, *De Legibus*, fol. 34. Maitland had observed the connection (*Bracton's Note Book*, ii.665n).
3. Sayles, *Select Cases in the Court of King's Bench*, i.xxvii–xxviii.

right to appeal to the king for a remedy and, since the king was constantly travelling about the country, the court before the king (*coram rege*) had to be peripatetic. But this court had ceased to exist after 1216 during the minority of Henry III and, though pleas were heard *coram rege* for some years before 1234, there was no regularly constituted king's bench until that year. So far as the exchequer was concerned, this had at one time been a court of common pleas as well as a financial tribunal, but the two sides were seen to have drifted apart by 1234, and there was no need to maintain a connexion between them when the justiciar, the head of both, disappeared.[4] The restructuring of 1234 was therefore the logical outcome of events: with the irretrievable loss of Normandy and the increasing complexity of administration, reforms could not long have been delayed.

Inevitably the new organisation of the courts and administrative departments affected the form and functions of parliament. With king's bench, common bench, exchequer, and chancery separately staffed with professional civil servants and lawyers and following a well-marked routine and keeping abundant records, a long step had been taken towards that sharp division between the various organs of government which is characteristic of the modern state. It is true that the king's bench and the chancery still followed the king and bore the characteristics of departments of the household, but the ties became looser and looser and the king developed within the household a more intimate organisation he could more directly control.[5] Over and above this scheme of administration stood the great council, already in 1236 termed parliament in an official record, thus depriving the chronicler Matthew Paris of the 'self-conscious innovation' in 1246 which has strangely been ascribed to him.[6] It was a superior court, to which business could be adjourned in order to secure a more considered opinion on some awkward point, where a decision could be ob-

4. Additional barons of the exchequer were appointed on 6 July (*Close Rolls, 1231–34*, pp. 569–70). The court of the exchequer of pleas consequently emerges: cf. Jenkinson and Fermoy, *Select Cases in the Exchequer of Pleas*, pp. liii, lxxxvii.
5. This evolution might, so T. F. Tout thought, be traced from 1234 (*Chapters in Medieval Administrative History*, i.239–43).
6. R. F. Treharne in *English Hist. Review*, lxxiv (1959), 592.

tained that a minister or judge hesitated to take on his own initiative. In parliament the chancellor, the treasurer, the judges of the two benches, the barons of the exchequer, and other ministers of the king will have their place, side by side with the magnates. In parliament the highest wisdom, the collective wisdom, of the land is concentrated, a wisdom contributed far more by the ministers and judges than by the magnates, who —if we except the bishops with a ministerial career behind them—were now finding the techniques of government too complicated and, indeed, had no desire to be trammelled by them.

We must not get involved in a long and tedious narrative of details, but it is essential to say something of the meetings immediately after the reforms had been instituted. At Michaelmas 1234 a council assembled at Westminster and by good fortune we have the names of the magnates present, forty-three in all: the archbishop of Canterbury and ten bishops, ten earls, and twenty-two barons, headed by Simon de Montfort, who was not yet recognised as earl of Leicester. There were others in attendance, and we can be confident that they were justices or ministers or minor officials: indeed, we can be sure that the newly created king's bench, at least, was represented, for the fullest record of the proceedings is on the king's bench roll. There were three major matters the council had to consider: special bastardy; the application of two methods of legal procedure, that is, the assize of *darrein presentment* to ecclesiastical prebends and the assize *utrum* to appropriated churches; and the interpretation of chapter 42 of the Great Charter of 1217, which limited the number of lawful meetings of county courts and hundred courts. The question of special bastardy provides us with an admirable illustration of the intricacies of legal dispute and the need for a general discussion to settle them. For children born out of wedlock were legitimate at canon law if their parents subsequently married. But should they be regarded as legitimate at common law and thereby entitled to succeed to their fathers' property? And if a marriage had to be proved, would this be a matter for an ecclesiastical court or a royal court? It was eventually decided in the council of Merton in 1236 that they could not be regarded as legitimate at common law, and this remained the rule in England until 1926, when the canon law view prevailed. All the business to be transacted in 1234 was what we should call today government business, business that had arisen because in the work of the courts difficulty had been experienced in interpreting the law, and the basis of discussion was in each case a proposal presumably put forward by the judges. Like future parliaments, the council is sitting to resolve judicial doubts.

The council of Merton in January 1236 was responsible for the so-called Statute of Merton, the earliest statute now to be found upon the statute roll. Most of its provisions concern the rights of landowners and their heirs. According to the preamble, this legislation was "provided' by the magnates and 'conceded' by the king. We are thus going beyond the point where the king legislates 'by common counsel of our baronage' (*communi consilio baronagii nostri*): the Statute of Merton incorporated the wishes of the barons after long argument and debate and it was not, therefore, it should be observed, solely a government measure.

The next council of which we have detailed knowledge took place a year after that at Merton. It appears to have opened at Westminster on 20 January 1237 and to have continued until 5 February. In composition this council seems to have been very much like the Merton council and was attended by archbishops, bishops, abbots, and priors and by earls and barons: it is called a 'general council' or a 'great council' by the chroniclers, but what it is important for us to note is that it is termed a 'parliament' on the records of a court of law in 1236, soon after the changes of 1234 had been made.[7] The parliament is evidently so called by a royal clerk because the expression is beginning to acquire a technical meaning. It is a special meeting, an afforced meeting of the king's council in which 'discussion' is paramount and decision or judgement an incidental thereof. To it the justice or justices of the king's bench knew that they could refer for consideration one of the cases before them in which the king had expressed an interest. Other business was put forward by the government: legislation

7. Richardson and Sayles, 'The Earliest Known Official Use of the Term "Parliament" ', *English Hist. Review*, lxxxii (1967), 747–50. Cf. J. A. Watt, 'The First Recorded Use of the Word "Parliament" in Ireland', *Irish Jurist*, iv (1969), 123–26, where it is thought to be found on an Irish pipe roll of 1235.

concerning the royal forests and changes in the dates from which several forms of action at law could be brought. The overriding purpose of the council was to consider the king's demand for an aid. He obtained a grant, amounting to a thirtieth of personal property, as consideration for his confirmation of the charters. This parliament presents, then, features which have been regarded as characteristic of parliaments as they evolved under Edward I and, indeed, are features of some of them—legislation, taxation, the confirmation of the Great Charter. But as in those parliaments, simple grievances were considered and it has never been adequately realised that routine and relatively unimportant matters were also being discussed at parliaments, matters which it was rarely worth while recording [8] because a place on the files of departments and courts was deemed adequate.

The word 'parliament' is used again in 1242 quite casually in the English chancery.[9] An entry on the close roll tells us that the justice of the forest had been informed that John de Neville was to be permitted to retain his bailiwick until the king's parliament, which was to be held in London a month after Midsummer. If this parliament ever met—and since the king was out of the country on the date appointed, we think it doubtful—no other business transacted there is recorded. But we would nevertheless stress the importance of this entry, for it is one of the few early notices of relatively unimportant matters discussed at great councils or parliaments. And though we have said that this entry is the first in which 'parliament' is mentioned on a chancery roll, we should not overlook a previous entry in this same year which speaks of a 'colloquium', the more elegant synonym for 'parliament'.[10] This is the description given to a great council in London late in January to which bishops, abbots, earls, and barons had been summoned. So far as we know, its purpose was financial. An aid was sought from the magnates and the levy of a scutage at the rate of three marks a knight's fee was approved. There seems, however, a possibility that it was at this meeting that the well-

8. A dispute concerning the services due to the honour of Peveril in Northamptonshire was also considered in 1237 (*Close Rolls, 1234–37*, p. 399).

9. *Close Rolls, 1237–42*, p. 447.

10. *Ibid.*, p. 431.

known ordinance for watch and ward was discussed, though the date of the writs communicating this ordinance to the counties, namely 24 May, is certainly considerably later than the date of the council at which its provisions may have been settled.[11]

For no obvious reason we learn very little of parliaments or great councils for some years after 1242. The king was absent from the country until late in September 1243. The regent, Walter Gray, archbishop of York, held an important council at Rochester on 9 September 1242,[12] but thereafter, though great councils were presumably resumed with the king's return to England, we have but casual and intermittent notices of them. An aid to marry the king's eldest daughter was granted in February 1245 by common counsel of the magnates of England (*per commune consilium magnatum Anglie*),[13] and there is a reference to a meeting of magnates at Westminster on the occasion of the Whitsuntide festival in the same year.[14] Again, in September 1246 there is a reference to the advice given by the magnates (*de communi consilio regis*) that the common law of England should apply to Ireland and that all writs of course should be available there under the kings' new seal.[15] Failing these casual entries in the chancery and the exchequer, we should hardly guess that great councils continued to meet; and then, by one of the vagaries of enrolment which are so puzzling at this period, we get a sudden crop of references to the parliament *eo nomine* that met at Westminster on the Octave of Candlemas (9 February) in 1248.

There is nothing to suggest that this was a particularly important assembly. It happened that the awkward matter of a papal grant to the archbishop of Canterbury arose and that the magnates refused their consent to diverting a year's revenue from vacant churches in their gift: but this was not a major question.[16] No other entry on the rolls refers to a matter even of this moment, only to matters of small importance, even

11. *Ibid.*, pp. 482ff.
12. *Ibid.*, pp. 466ff.
13. Madox, *History of the Exchequer*, i.593, *n.* d.
14. *Close Rolls, 1242–47*, p. 357.
15. *Foedera*, i.266; *Cal. Patent Rolls, 1232–47*, p. 488.
16. *Close Rolls, 1247–51*, p. 109.

trivialities. The chief justice of the bench is instructed to postpone a distress until this parliament; [17] while other distresses
and a demand for payment are postponed in like manner by the
barons of the exchequer.[18] From another entry we learn that
an unlawful outlawry was annulled in the king's court, before
the king and the whole parliament.[19] As we have seen, there
are stray indications that minor and personal matters have been
coming before great councils and parliaments, but the entries
relating to the Candlemas parliament of 1248 go a long way to
confirm us in the view that the king's ministers and judges
had for some time been transferring problems to parliament for
discussion and decision. And then, oddly enough it may
seem, for some years such entries cease, and after 1248 there is
a large gap in the information concerning parliament contained
in the chancery and exchequer rolls, which appear to ignore
it until 1254. From other sources we learn that a parliament
met on 28 April 1252 in the refectory of Westminster Abbey.[20] Here on 9 May Simon de Montfort, who had for some
years been governing Gascony, still part of the king's dominions, on the king's behalf, confronted the aggrieved Gascons
who had suffered under his rule. Although there was in no
strict sense a trial, the charges against Simon and his counter-
charges give the confrontation much of the aspect of one. The
charges were based upon written complaints, a number of
which have come down to us.[21] Important as this episode was,
it is difficult to believe that it occupied the whole time that
this parliament was in session, but of other business we know
nothing.

A parliament that met a year later in May 1253 is also of
importance. The purpose of summoning it was to obtain funds
for the king's expedition to Gascony. The barons responded
by granting an aid for knighting the king's eldest son.[22] The

17. *Ibid.*, p. 104.
18. L. T. R. Memoranda Roll, no. 20 (32 Henry III), ms. 4, 13.
19. *Close Rolls, 1247–51*, p. 107.
20. Bémont, *Simon de Montfort* (1884), pp. 340ff.
21. *Royal Letters of Henry III*, ii.72–76; Bémont, *op. cit.*, pp. 279–31.
22. Matthew Paris, *Chronica Majora*, v.377; *Red Book of the Exchequer*, iii.1064.

bishops seem to have made difficulty about a subsidy. Certainly an impressive ceremony was arranged for 13 May, when sentence of excommunication was pronounced upon violators of the charters and, since this ceremony took place in Westminster Hall, its connection with the parliament seems obvious. The king had, however, obtained very little financial assistance towards his expensive campaign in Gascony, and the regents he had left behind him, the queen and Richard of Cornwall, assembled an afforced council—it seems nowhere to be called a parliament—that met at Westminster on 27 January 1254, in order to obtain a grant from the laity and apparently to obtain a clerical subsidy. The bishops expressed themselves prepared to make a personal grant, in the unlikely contingency that the king of Castile invaded Gascony, but offered no prospect of any special subsidy from the clergy at large. The barons offered their personal services in the event of an invasion of Gascony, but no money.[23] Without very much hope, the regents summoned a parliament to meet at Westminster on 26 April, and they took the extraordinary step of summoning delegates (*nuncii*) from the lower clergy and two knights from every shire to represent the county court.[24] At the same time they warned the king that there was no prospect of aid from the laity unless he wrote to the regents themselves, charging them to see that the charters were strictly observed, and in the same sense to the sheriffs requiring them to make public proclamation accordingly. There were many complaints, the regents added, that the sheriffs and other royal bailiffs did not observe the charters.[25] It is beyond doubt that the regents obtained no aid for the king. Of the doings of the clerical delegates a contemporary account has fortunately come down to us. They offered a grant on terms which proved unacceptable. But one of the terms is especially notable: it was that the king should confirm the liberties of the Church as set out in the great Charter

23. *Close Rolls, 1253–54,* pp. 107, 111–12.
24. Ibid., pp. 114–116. This assembly is termed 'parliament' in the writ to the bishop-elect of Lincoln, excusing him from attendance and permitting him to send proctors (*ibid.,* p. 43), and also in a note regarding the collection of the crusading tenth (*Cal. Patent Rolls, 1247–58,* p. 370).
25. *Royal Letters of Henry III,* ii.102–3.

and in articles that the bishops had drawn up the previous year.[26] This parliament is, of course, a precedent for summoning to parliament representatives of the shires and the lower clergy, and on that aspect we shall have occasion to comment later. But it may be well to say at this point that there is nothing to suggest that the regents had any idea that they were making history, nothing to suggest that, in what they did, they acted in consultation with the king. They were in great perplexity and any device they adopted to raise money for the king—devices that proved fruitless—could have carried no implication for the future. There appears to be no evidence that any business other than financial was discussed at this parliament; but at another which met at Oxford, after a short interval, on 19 July in this year of 1254, called primarily to discuss the situation in Gascony, there seems no doubt that minor matters were considered—in particular, amercements imposed upon the citizens of London in respect of the exchange.[27] Again, in the following year, at the parliament that was summoned in the Easter term principally for financial business, there were considered not only the exemption to be given to poor religious houses from the crusading tenth,[28] but also the conflicting claims to a great fish asserted by both the king and the bishop of Norwich.[29]

We have now brought our narrative up nearly to the year 1258, when parliament was to be enshrined within a written constitution. It will be realised that it is only exceptionally that we are in possession of detailed information relating to any great council or parliament:[30] still, we know enough to see that we cannot at this period draw a clear distinction between the one and the other. The name of parliament is as yet hardly recognised as a formal title, and though it is more and more freely accorded to these assemblies of magnates, it does not

26. Printed W. E. Lunt in *Persecution and Liberty*, pp. 140–41.
27. L. T. R. Memoranda Roll, no. 29 (38 Henry III), m. 17.
28. *Cal. Patent Rolls, 1247–58*, p. 399.
29. L. T. R. Memoranda Roll, no. 30 (39 Henry III), m. 10.
30. Some information will be found in chronicles mentioned in Parry, *Parliaments and Councils of England*. Note Arnold fitz Thedmar's chronicle in *Liber de Antiquis Legibus*, pp. 25–26, which related how the king adjourned to the parliament at Mid-Lent 1257 a dispute regarding the franchises of the city of London.

occur in such few writs of summons as have survived.[31] A man is not yet expressly summoned to "parliament'. It would seem, however, as though a formal summons to bishops, earls, and barons who were on the king's council was recognized as a summons to parliament even though that word did not occur in the writ.[32] Apart from them and the king's ministerial counsellors, there were no other constituents of parliament, though towards the end of the period abbots, as well as bishops, are sometimes summoned; but this, it would seem, is only when the king proposes to demand financial aid. He was not, however, anxious for their personal appearance, and the presence of a fellow-monk with power to assent to a grant was equally satisfactory.[33] Questions of finance seem, however, to have occupied the time of these assemblies but infrequently. It is common ground with those who have investigated the problem of taxation under Henry III that he was not often successful in persuading bishops and barons to grant a subsidy, though the grant of customary aids and scutages could not be avoided.[34] This does not necessarily mean that a good deal of time might not have been occupied in negotiations that came to nothing, but we have no evidence that this was the case. Again, legislation was intermittent. What then occupied the magnates at these assemblies? They were, of course, as parliaments continued to be, social occasions, but, like later parliaments, more than that. The difficulty is to guess—we can do no more than guess—the extent to which administrative questions were discussed. It seems impossible to suppose that such scattered and sparse notes as we have on the rolls of the chancery and the exchequer represent the full volume of business of this character. Rather we would suggest that enrolling clerks regarded it

31. A writ for a meeting in 1242 and three writs for meetings in 1254 are on the close rolls and have been printed in *Lords Reports*, iii.7, 12–13, and in *Close Rolls*, 1237–42, p. 428; 1251–54, pp. 107, 114–15, 140–41. See also the writ mentioned in the next note.

32. See the writ to the abbot of St. Albans and the note added to it, presumably by Matthew Paris, *Chronica Majora*, vi. (Additamenta), 392.

33. *Close Rolls*, 1237–42, p. 431.

34. The incidence of taxation under Henry III is conveniently shown in the tables printed by J. H. Ramsay, *History of the Revenue of the Kings of England*, i.363–64. Details are given by Mitchell, *Taxation in Medieval England*, pp. 119–209.

as too trivial to be worth recording.[35] The little of which we have knowledge seems to be no more than a sample, but upon such a question he would be a bold man who would express a confident opinion.

35. For example, see the letter to the bishop-elect of Lincoln of 2 April 1254, authorising him to send proctors to the parliament at Easter (*Close Rolls*, 1253–54, p. 43). This clearly implies a writ of summons to the bishops.

4. The Provisions of Oxford and Their Consequences

When we seek for the remote origins of ancient institutions we can hardly ever give a date or find a specific act of creation. If we have seen signs that afforced meetings of the king's council had assumed greater significance after 1234 in the administration of the country, it is not through forgetting that such meetings reach further back into the past. But there is no room for doubt that the year 1258 marks the date of the conception of organised parliaments in England. As we have said, parliament was of itself no innovation, though our knowledge before 1258 is so fragmentary that we find it difficult to differentiate parliaments clearly from all other afforced sessions of the king's council. But the Provisions of Oxford alone show that contemporaries at least were not in doubt: to them parliament was a well-understood institution. 'Let it be remembered that there are to be three parliaments a year: the first at the Octave of Michaelmas (6 October), the second on the Morrow of Candlemas (3 February) and the third on the first day of June.' These are the words of responsible men who are initiating solemn changes in the future governance of the realm and making parliament an established part of the machinery of administration. To them parliament could not have been vague and indeterminate. And forty years later an English lawyer sees no difficulty in defining parliament. His qualifications to speak are impeccable, for he not only introduced order into the chaos in which Bracton had left the manuscript of his treatise on the common law but he brought Bracton's work up to date in the light of a new phenomenon, the statute law, of which Bracton knew little. 'The king', says the author of *Fleta*, 'has his court in his council in his parliaments when prelates, earls, barons, magnates and others learned in the law are present. And doubts are determined there regarding judgements, new remedies are devised for wrongs newly brought to light, and there also justice is dispensed to everyone according to his deserts.'[1] Of course, between 1258 and the close of the century there will be much change and modification, but the purpose was all in the direction of creating a more efficient instrument of administration and justice, not a precocious form of parliamentary democracy.

The Oxford parliament stands out among all the parliaments of the thirteenth century as the most significant, and for that reason it is essential that we should tarry a while with it. To a London chronicler[2] it was 'that distinguished parliament' (*illud insigne parliamentum*), but a later hand, more royalist than grammatical, changed the adjective *insigne* to *insane*,[3] and so the parliament of Oxford became known in the nineteenth century as the 'Mad Parliament'. And maybe, as we look at what it did, though we may regard its aspirations as distinguished, we may well think its methods, impracticable as they were, as not a little mad.

By the beginning of 1258 Henry III's financial position had become hopeless. To his dying day he was an utterly reckless spender, and his hare-brained scheme to obtain the crown of Sicily for his son Edmund brought him face to face with bankruptcy when he found that he could not provide the sums of money he had agreed to pay the pope. The Sicilian adventure forms a part of the background to the events of 1258, but there was another part: whatever efforts the king's ministers and judges had made in order to widen the scope of justice and to enforce it, they could not depend on steady support from

1. *Fleta*, ed. Richardson and Sayles, ii. 109.
2. *Liber de Antiquis Legibus* (1846), p. 37.
3. Correctly it should be *insanum*. *English Hist. Review*, xl. 402: see the facsimile in *Bull. Inst. Hist. Research*, iii (1925–26), p. 110.

the king himself. Many of the magnates themselves were determined to obtain effective measures of reform before they
consented to come to the assistance of the feckless king. In his
financial desperation the king had summoned a parliament
to meet at Westminster after Easter on 9 April. After
much argument the king had brought himself to concede the
baronial demand for reform in return for an assurance of
financial help. The agreement is embodied in two separate
instruments, dated 2 May, and only in the light of what they
contain can the proceedings of the parliament of Oxford be
understood. The first of the two instruments stated that, if the
king ordered the state of the realm to be reformed in accordance with the advice of his barons and if the pope modified
his demands in regard to Sicily, then the magnates would
guarantee a general aid for the king. The king therefore agreed
that by Christmas he would introduce reforms by counsel of his
barons and that he would faithfully observe what was ordained. As proof he submitted himself to ecclesiastical censure: that is, if he failed to keep his word, he would be liable
to the penalty of excommunication.[4] The second instrument
embodied the king's agreement, under oath, that the state of
the realm should be rectified and reformed by a body of
twenty-four, made up of twelve of the king's council and
twelve elected by the magnates, who were to meet at Oxford
on 11 June. Whatever was ordained by a majority of the
Twenty-four the king swore to observe.[5] For their part, the
earls and barons promised to do their best to secure a general
aid when the work of the Twenty-four had been completed.
Shortly afterwards writs of summons must have been issued for
a meeting of parliament at Oxford where the Twenty-four
could put forward their suggestions.

The instruments of 2 May highlight the mistrust between
the barons and the king. Despite his promises the king clearly
resented the coercion applied to him. The immediate outcome of this mutual antipathy was ominous. The king called
upon his friends to come to the assembly at Oxford accompanied by their armed retainers, and a party of Burgundian

4. *Foedera*, i.370.
5. *Ibid.*, 371.

knights and their followers, who had been engaged for a campaign in Wales, were diverted to Oxford on 25 May.[6] These preparations for a conflict inevitably became known. In self-defence the reforming barons summoned their own followers to appear in arms: they had the excuse of the prospective war against the Welsh.[7] The king did not assemble his forces at Oxford because of a threat from the barons. Simon de Montfort, the king's brother-in-law and his most forthright critic, had supplied most of the driving-power to the opposition, but he was absent in France with other baronial leaders nearly the whole of the time between the end of the Easter parliament and the parliament at Oxford. The onus rests upon the king for stupidly converting into an armed camp the city in which the parliament and the Twenty-four were to meet to engage in the stupendous task of reforming the realm.[8]

Despite the tense atmosphere the Twenty-four set to work upon a scheme of reform. Some of the barons appear to have already drawn up a schedule setting out the matters of law and administration which, in their view, needed amendment: this document has come down to us and is known as the Petition of the Barons.[9] The Twenty-four were engaged in what we should call constitutional reconstruction, and their proposals fell under three heads: the appointment and control of the principal ministers; the king's council; parliament.[10]

The Twenty-four decided to resurrect the office of justiciar, with specialist functions rather than the general authority previously enjoyed.[11] The justiciar would *ex officio* be a leading member of the council but his work was now to be primarily judicial. It was his duty to remove the errors and correct the wrongdoings of all subordinate justices and bailiffs, not only those of the king but also those of earls, barons, and others: that is to say, his was to be a court of appeal from all other

6. *Close Rolls, 1256–59*, pp. 223f.
7. Bémont, *Simon de Montfort*, pp. 327f.
8. Parliament was in session on, or very shortly before, 11 June.
9. 'Annals of Burton', in *Annales Monastici*, i.439–43.
10. See the 'Provisions of Oxford' in the version given in the *Annals of Burton*, pp. 446–53 and the version of an abridged text, published by Richardson and Sayles, 'The Provisions of Oxford', *Bull. John Rylands Library*, xvii (1933), 291–321.
11. See above, p. 28.

courts within the realm. He was to hold office for one year only and then be answerable for his conduct of affairs before the king's council. This was a most serious departure from previous practice, for it placed at the head of the judiciary a minister virtually independent of the king. The justiciar's authority was widened by elaborate arrangements for the encouragement and hearing of all complaints of injustice. Similarly the treasurer and the chancellor were not to take direct orders from the king and were to be appointed for one year and answer thereafter for what they had done. Since all revenue was to be paid in at the exchequer, there was complete centralisation and control of the royal finances, and the king was prevented from intercepting revenue for his own capricious spending. Some thought was given to subordinate officers like the escheators and the most important of local officers, the sheriffs, who were to be appointed annually from substantial landowners resident within the shire. The over-all plan is clear. Apart from what we nowadays would call the permanent civil service, officials at headquarters and in the localities were not to remain in office for more than a year without close scrutiny of their behaviour and competence.

To make this reform effective it was all-important to ensure that the counsellors in attendance upon the king were men of independent judgement and not royal tools. Though the sole executive was to be, at least nominally, the king, the English monarchy was to be impersonal, freed as much as possible from the king's personal whims. In the England of the thirteenth century it was recognised that, though the king had no peer, he was under the law and must respect its provisions. Moreover, he must act by the advice of the baronage, a doctrine with which all concerned were well acquainted. But though nobles and lawyers might cherish this concept of monarchy, its implications, when spelt out and set down in black and white, were not likely to be acceptable to Henry III.

Elaborate and intricate arrangements were made for the council that was to advise and, in effect, to control the king. The Twenty-four proceeded to elect the counsellors in characteristic medieval fashion. The twelve who represented the king chose two members of the twelve representing the barons

—and the barons, it is to be noted, are called the 'community' or 'commune'. The baronial twelve, in turn, chose two of the king's twelve representatives. The four constituted a committee to choose the counsellors. The names of those elected were then submitted to the Twenty-four for approval. Fifteen counsellors in all were selected by this method, which, as it turned out, gave a majority to the baronial representatives. The general duties of the Fifteen as counsellors were to advise the king constantly on all matters for the purpose of amending anything that required to be redressed. In parliament they were to survey the state of the realm and to consider 'matters affecting both the king and the realm' (*les communes busoignes du roy et du reaume*): which is equivalent to what we would call 'public affairs'. With matters affecting the king personally, parliament at least had no concern.

It should be observed that the Fifteen did not constitute the whole of the king's council, though the intention was clearly that they should dominate it. It always needed the presence and expert advice of the justiciar, the chancellor, and the treasurer, and, in a measure, of the judges, but also of other ministers when matters concerning them came up for discussion. There was not, nor was there intended to be, any breach with the past: from the baronial point of view the council was strengthened but not essentially altered. Nor was the king precluded from calling to his council his intimate advisers: for example, his eldest son, Edward.

The Fifteen were to control the council, but it was out of the question, nor could it ever have been contemplated, that the Fifteen, as a body, should be, day in day out, in attendance upon the king. The difficulty would be to ensure their attendance when their presence was required. Therefore, to avoid the delays and embarrassments that might result from the absence of many of them, the procedure of the council was clarified and regulated at the Michaelmas parliament of 1259. The Fifteen were to be represented at the routine meetings of the council by two or three of their number. These counsellors were to be of middling status (*mesne gent*), words that would exclude earls and bishops from tedious and time-consuming work, and they were to be present at the council for a specific purpose. Their invidious task was to decide

whether any weighty affair (*grand busoigne*) that might arise
could be decided by their advice or could be delayed until the
next parliament, or, if it could not be delayed, whether it
justified summoning by writ the whole of the Fifteen.[12] Here
we have an explanation of an otherwise unexplained term in
the minutes of the decisions taken at Oxford. The chancellor
had been required to swear that he would not seal any important grant without the assent of the 'great council' (*grant
conseil*) or the majority of them. The only possible meaning
of 'great council' in this context is the Fifteen. The councils
which all or the greater part of the Fifteen attended would be
'great' councils, as contrasted with the small councils, required for routine business, which were attended by two or
three of their number. We must not suppose that the 'great
council' was the normal designation of the Fifteen: it is no
more than the shorthand language of an informal minute by
a clerk. What is of interest is the use of the term in 1258, for
we rarely come across it in the surviving documents of the
thirteenth century: it is not until after the reign of Edward
I that 'great council' will become an expression in common
usage.

The plan of the Twenty-four for the reform of parliament
can be understood only against the historical background of
parliament. They conceived their task not as one of creating a
new instrument of government but as one of making an existing
instrument more effective. As we have seen, parliament was
becoming the name given to some afforced meetings of the
council, though not to all such meetings. The Twenty-four
proceeded to give parliament an authority, a status, superior
to that of other afforced sessions of the council, and they
gave it definition by requiring that it should meet three times
a year at stated dates (such periodicity implies definition),
that it should have a definite constitution, and that certain
definite functions should be assigned to it. The Twenty-four
did not need to say that parliament was the afforced meeting
of the king's council, but they thought it desirable to state
expressly that the Fifteen should be present and that in parliament they were to survey the state of the realm and to con-

12. *Annales Monastici,* i. 477.

sider any matters touching the king in his public capacity and the country at large. The terms of reference were not in any way restrictive, as is clear enough from what we learn of the actual work of parliament at this period. At this very parliament, for instance, an action that had been removed from the court of common pleas in Dublin was heard in the presence, among others, of earls and barons.[13] We have seen something of the business that was coming before parliament in the years before 1258. Quite obviously there was every intention that this parliamentary business should continue: it all formed part of the contemporary conception of parliament.[14]

When we ask who were to afforce the king's council in parliaments, the obvious answer is 'the baronage', or, as it was known at the time, the *communitas*, the *commune*. But while the baronage might be described in such general terms, it defied definition and a general summons of this vague body was impracticable and in any case attendance at three parliaments a year would have been intolerably burdensome. The Twenty-four hit upon the expedient of asking the barons assembled

13. Curia Regis Roll, no. 158 (Trinity 1258), m. 12.

14. It is common to seek resemblances at this time between the parliament in England and the parliament of Paris, and it is manifestly true that many English nobles and officials were well conversant with the French *parlement*: indeed, after the peace treaty of 1259, the king of England in his capacity as duke of Aquitaine had to be represented there by proctors who were usually English civil servants. But the surface similarities conceal a fundamental difference. The French parliament had not evolved as the English parliament had done, from meetings of the council, whatever form they took and whatever their regularity, for discussion with subjects. Instead it had been instituted shortly before 1250 by St. Louis, the French king, to meet in ordered sessions to cope with demands for justice that were, in England, being satisfied by the three courts of common law, king's bench, common bench, and exchequer of pleas. Though the French parliament did discuss public affairs, the bulk of its business was judicial and it heard many appeals from the courts of feudatories. Louis IX had therefore taken a step in France in the second half of the thirteenth century which was very similar to that taken by Henry II in the second half of the twelfth century in weakening the powers of feudatories and reforming the administration of justice. In England the result had been the creation of eyre courts in the localities and other courts at headquarters. France had nothing to correspond and their work had perforce to be done by the French parliament. From these duties it could never dissociate itself, as the English parliament tended in time to do, and we must bear this difference in mind when we consider the evolution of parliament in England and in France.

at Oxford to choose twelve representatives who would attend the three regular parliaments and any other specially summoned meetings. The assent of these twelve would bind the whole of the *commune*. There was no intention of limiting attendance: the sole purpose of this provision was to secure a minimum representative attendance. The result was, of course, to give parliament very much the same aspect as it had before 1258. It was predominantly a meeting of magnates. And while three parliaments a year were envisaged, in exceptional circumstances a fourth parliament might be summoned, as happened in 1260. And there might be other councils of varying composition, which met at other times than parliament and were not parliaments.

Such was the constitutional framework that the Twenty-four erected, but there was one administrative reform devised at Oxford which is of major importance, a procedure for trying the complaints of the people in general, a reform linked with the resuscitation of the office of justiciar. A good deal of responsibility for it rested upon the *commune* of England, that is, the barons who attended the parliament. An open letter of 22 February 1259, circulated by the council and the twelve who had been 'chosen by the commune of England',[15] indicates that the 'commune' helped to devise the scheme whereby four knights were appointed in each county to enrol complaints of trespasses and other wrongs in preparation for the arrival of the justiciar. We shall see later how this reform influenced the direction followed by parliament early in the reign of Edward I.

Ever since the unhappy beginnings of Henry III's reign the courts had in the opinion of contempories been failing to provide justice. It is true that complaints against the oppressions and wrongdoings of those in authority had been heard before justices in eyre in the sessions they held occasionally in such counties as they visited, but it was highly desirable that years should not pass before justice was seen to be done. But attempts to strengthen the administration of the law had evidently not been conspicuously successful before 1258. Indeed, the king was often, through his officials, the worst of all offenders. Outcries against oppression continued and multiplied, as is

15. *Foedera*, i.381.

witnessed by the many demands that the Great Charter should be confirmed and observed. The situation had become beyond remedy by promises and empty exhortations on the part of the king: [16] the sheriffs and other local government officials were not likely to mend their ways except under compulsion. Therefore the king was pushed aside, and the arrangements for redressing popular grievances, which were outlined at Oxford, provided at long last practical ways and means of operation. The machinery for hearing and determining complaints of injustice took a good many months of trial and error to get into working order, and the various stages seem to have been threshed out at meetings of parliament. The proclamation of 20 October 1258, which encouraged the submission of complaints to the four knights appointed to receive them in each county,[17] must have been drawn up when the Michaelmas parliament was in session, while the open letter of 22 February 1259, which followed up this proclamation, was the outcome of the Candlemas parliament.[18] There was, however, in 1258 no thought that parliament itself was the appropriate place for hearing and determining complaints from all and sundry.

Parliaments were not normally engaged in initiating drastic reforms and it is well to bear in mind that the Oxford parliament preserved the characteristics of an ordinary parliament. We have already mentioned the appeal that came to the king from his court at Dublin.[19] The hearing apparently took place near the beginning of the parliament, on 16 June 'before the earls, barons and all the justices of England at the king's great parliament'. Other actions during this session of parliament were heard before the judges of the king's bench alone.[20] We shall see when we come to the reign of Edward I that the greater part of parliamentary business was transacted apart

16. L. T. R. Memoranda Roll, no. 25 (Henry III), m. 2: printed by Prynne, *Brief Animadversions* (1669), p. 53, and again by M. T. Clanchy, in *History*, liii (1968), 215f.

17. 'Annals of Burton', in *Annales Monastici*, i. 456–57; *Foedera*, i.375.

18. *Foedera*, i.381.

19. See n. 13 above.

20. For example, an action by the king against the earl of Surrey, begun on 25 June, was assuredly started in the Oxford parliament (*Close Rolls, 1256–59*, p. 302).

from plenary or public sessions. Whether the knighting of one of the king's squires at Oxford 'in parliament' took place in a plenary session we have no means of knowing: [21] but in any case this incident illustrates another aspect, the social aspect of parliament, which was to grow in prominence with the years. Yet another aspect is illustrated when the fixing of the price at which Alice, the widow of Edmund de Lacy, was to have the custody of her late husband's lands was deferred until the king could have the advice of his council which was about to meet at Oxford: the council is, of course, the council in parliament.[22] And finally we may note that Llewelyn, against whom war was threatened, had a safeguard 'to this our parliament of Oxford', obviously to treat of peace.[23]

The recital of these casual items of parliamentary business may serve to put the parliament of Oxford in perspective. Though it began and ended in dramatic fashion, its proceedings were far from being all drama. Nor have we any reason to suppose that the few minor matters to which a reference has been preserved were more than a fraction of like business that was expected to be transacted at this as at other parliaments. The session had lasted little more than a fortnight and some business, left unfinished at Oxford, seems to have been continued at Winchester in the early days of July. By 4 August the Twenty-four had been disbanded and their task handed over to the fifteen elected members of the council. Still, what had been done in that fortnight at Oxford was, indeed, memorable. Both the action immediately taken and the proposals for future action were alarming to the privileged and the conservative, both in Church and State, and they cast long shadows before them. For the reforming barons had, in modern terms, gained control of both the executive and the legislature and, unless there was to be a counter-revolution, it was their will that would henceforth prevail.

Like the Great Charter of 1215, the Provisions of Oxford of 1258 were the work of angry and fearful men, and anger and fear are bad counsellors and do not incline to compromise. Yet the reforms they initiated show beyond doubt that they had

21. *Close Rolls*, 1256–58, p. 229.
22. *Cal. Patent Rolls*, 1247–58, p. 632.
23. *Foedera*, i.372; *Cal. Patent Rolls*, 1247–58, p. 632.

it firmly in mind to vindicate the law and to protect established rights. But they were confronted by a problem to which
they had no answer in the terms of practical politics. What
guarantee could they provide against future misconduct by the
king or those who acted under his orders? If the king did
wrong, he could not, save by his rarely given permission, be
sued by his own writs in his own courts, and the petition of
right was as yet in its early infancy. And even if the petition of
right were to be given the widest possible extension, it would
cover wrongs done to individuals only and not render jus-
ticiable the wrongs done to subjects as a whole by the invasion
of their constitutional rights (if we may venture the modern
phraseology). Henry III was, of course, bound to observe the
terms of the Great Charter, which he had so often and so
publicly confirmed, and to respect his coronation oath. But
he was bound only in conscience and if it did not move him
or if its faint stirrings could be set at rest by futile gestures of
piety, then *in extremis* there was only one sanction his out-
raged subjects could apply: rebellion. That this was averted in
1258 is to the credit of the barons, not of the king. But in
their search for an alternative to rebellion, they could select
only from institutions of which they had experience. To control the council in and out of parliament was to control the
king. This was nothing original, nothing revolutionary, but the
enforcement of the ancient principle that the king must govern
by the advice of his barons. But that principle was pressed
further than ever before and the result in substance was to
revert to government by council as in the days of tutelage when
Henry III was a minor. But now the king was a grown man
and his tutors were to be not caretakers but a committee of
sorely tried and aggrieved barons.

It is hard to guess what was in the king's mind when he
agreed to the parliament which was, in his own words, to be
responsible for the reformation of the realm. He himself did
not plan reform: he submitted to it, or professed to do so, as
the price of a subsidy. But quite early he conceived a deep
hatred for the Provisions of Oxford, partly because he was
inherently insincere but mainly because he felt that he had
been outwitted, and not only outwitted but humiliated. Not
only Henry but the whole royal circle appears to have been

surprised and angered by the extremes to which the reforming barons went. Perhaps the king's advisers believed that a show of strength at the outset at Oxford would keep reforms within bounds; they may have hoped that the balancing of the reformers by an equal number of the king's friends among the Twenty-four would compel moderation. But the king's representatives were impelled to go further along the path of reform than the king would approve. Certainly the king and his relatives were aghast at the new model of government he had pledged himself to accept. And there were unfortunate grounds for his exasperation, for the barons went beyond broad changes in government and coupled them with humiliating interference with the private household, purging it not only of its senior members, the stewards, but of menials like the cooks. Henry could hardly forget that he was being treated like a cipher even within his own house.

Parliament was the testing ground where the king and the barons could try out their respective strengths. The barons in 1258 acknowledged the value and, indeed, indispensability of an institution they had known so long. They adopted and recognised it as the expression of supreme authority. Neither king nor barons were in dispute about its functions: they were to be in the future what they had been in the past. High politics, public affairs, call them what we will, like foreign commitments, legislation, taxation, had been discussed in parliaments long before 1258, as they would be ever afterwards, and no contemporary thought it worth while to prove the obvious. What was novel was the regularity with which parliament sat after Midsummer 1258, even though circumstances sometimes made it difficult to observe faithfully the dates for meeting laid down in the Provisions. It is sufficient merely to enumerate the parliaments before May 1262 when the king publicly repudiated the Provisions of Oxford. The list speaks for itself: Michaelmas 1258; Candlemas, Easter, and Michaelmas 1259; Candlemas, Easter, Midsummer, and Michaelmas 1260; Candlemas and September 1261; Candlemas 1262. Eleven parliaments in just over three and a quarter years. Similarly, Simon de Montfort for his part summoned three parliaments during the twelve months he was in power: Midsummer 1264, January and June 1265. The barons assumed that parliament would continue to meet, irrespective of the king's summons or the king's presence: indeed, the Provisions of Oxford had made no arrangements for formal summons of the barons, but the Fifteen and the Twelve were to be there as of right and their presence was sufficient for a properly constituted parliament. This was the most formidable challenge at the highest level to the king's authority and it was quite extraneous to and far above any question about the business of parliament. The king had to protest and insist that parliament could not meet save in his presence. But if he then chose not to be present, the baronial programme of reform would be destroyed. There was no avoiding a head-on collision if the king decided not to collaborate, and two incidents serve to throw a vivid light upon the insoluble dilemma.

In 1260 it was expected that there would be a parliament at Candlemas (2 February) and questions had been referred there for discussion.[24] Simon de Montfort and others had come to London to attend it. Whilst it was in session a letter arrived from the king, who was in France, stating that "it is not our will that any parliament should be held in our realm while we are absent, for this is improper and, so we believe, diminishes our honour'. He went on, however, to add that the justiciar of England was to continue to dispense justice to all and sundry, provided no new departure from the existing law was made 'unless we are there and give our assent'.[25] The justiciar, into whose keeping the country had been entrusted during the king's absence, told the barons that 'they should not have held a parliament until the king's arrival, which would be within three weeks.'[26] The barons accordingly adjourned parliament from day to day for three weeks, but the king did not return home until 23 April.

Eighteen months later a position was reached which would have been childishly ludicrous, had it not been fraught with such momentous consequences. The barons had arranged for a parliament to meet at St. Albans on 21 September 1261 and had ordered the attendance of three knights from each shire

24. *Close Rolls*, 1259–61, pp. 15, 17.
25. *Ibid.*, pp. 272–73; *Royal Letters of Henry III*, ii.153–55.
26. Bibliothèque Nationale MS. lat. 9016, no. 5: printed Bémont, *Simon de Montfort*, pp. 350–51.

'to discuss with them the common business of the kingdom'.
The king made a counter-move by requiring the knights to
come before him on the same day at Windsor.[27] It has often
been stated that no meeting took place at either St. Albans
or Windsor but, whether that is true or not, men had started
on their journeys. A hitherto unprinted letter underlines the
hopeless confusion:

> To his most dear friend Walter of Merton, the king's
> chancellor, Philip Basset,[28] greeting and sincere affection. We
> beseech you to tell the king the best way you can that he ought
> to dispatch his letters to Roger de Sumery [29] at Bradfield for
> the purpose of making him come to his parliament, just as he
> has instructed others to do, and this he should not fail to do.
> Because we have learned from the report of some that he intends
> to go to St. Albans if he does not previously receive a letter
> of summons from the king. Farewell.[30]

Civil war was scarcely avoidable. The details of the conflict
need not detain us here. In face of the king's opposition the
barons were driven to violence and the issue was decided at the
battle of Lewes in 1264 for the barons and at the battle of
Evesham in 1265 for the king. With the advantage of hindsight we can see that the reform programme was chimerical: it
demanded a quite unimaginable unity and constancy on the
part of the barons and an equally unimaginable resignation and
passivity on the part of the king and his friends. If the barons
did not get on with the king, he had only to bide his time:
they could not get on without him.

When the king came into his own again after Evesham,
parliament remained thereafter what it had been before.
There is no problem here: parliament had been the king's
creature and the fact that the reforming barons had adopted
and used it was no reason why it should be discarded—if it or
something like it could in fact have been done without. Therefore parliament continued to be convoked frequently: sixteen

27. *Close Rolls*, 1259–61, p. 490 (11 September 1261). Ten days
was inadequate for transmitting the writ and getting the knights to
Windsor.
28. The justiciar.
29. He was lord of the barony of Dudley and father-in-law of Ralph
Basset who was killed at Evesham in 1265.
30. Ancient Correspondence, vol. vii, no. 33.

parliaments met during the seven years 1265–72,[31] which compares not unfavourably with the three parliaments a year required in 1258. It is noticeable they were not often held during the troubled times—the three years after Evesham—and then never in London, which had so openly identified itself with anti-royalist sentiment. It was only after London had bought peace with the king in 1268 that he made it again the invariable meeting-place, the only exception being the parliament at Winchester in July 1270.[32]

There is nothing to indicate that knights of the shire or burgesses, to use a convenient term for borough representatives, were summoned to any of these sixteen parliaments. The king's parliaments were not connected in any way with county courts,[33] and we need only remind the reader that those who profess this belief are clearly not studying parliament as it appeared to contemporaries but the history of popular representation so beloved of nineteenth-century historians. It was no more than a matter of convenience in saving time and trouble that knights and burgesses had been occasionally summoned to headquarters to meet the council.[34] It had pleased the king's regents to summon knights to parliament in 1254; it had pleased the barons to summon them there at Michaelmas 1258 and in September 1261; it had pleased Simon de Montfort to summon them in June 1264 and again, this time with borough representatives, in January 1265 (but not to the parliament he convened for June 1265) in order to give as wide publicity as he could to the new form of government he had devised and

31. The list in the *Handbook of British Chronology* is based on printed evidence. We have supplemented and corrected it from manuscript sources.

32. *Handbook of British Chronology*, p. 506, queries the existence of this parliament, since only chronicle evidence could be cited. But it is authenticated from an official source (Curia Regis Rolls, no. 192 [Trinity 1270], m. 15).

33. R. F. Treharne in *English Hist. Review*, lxxiv (1959), 590: the 'rooting' of the English parliament, 'in the ancient community of the shire is, of course, not in dispute'.

34. See the article by A. B. White (cited below, p. 88) for many early examples of the consultation of groups through their representatives in a single central assembly, whether knights or Jews, moneyers or foresters. His remark (p. 739) that Stubbs was 'obsessed by the idea that the shire-moot was the prototype in little of the House of Commons' was a salutary warning sixty years ago that has been sadly ignored.

intended to put into operation. There is nothing very noteworthy in this except that it has been found so noteworthy,
and no contemporary chronicler thought it worth while to comment on their presence or absence at parliament. And when
Henry III himself summoned borough representatives to meet
him in 1268, he met them on their own when no parliament
was assembled.[35] In sum, between 1258 and 1272 some thirty-
four parliaments assembled: knights were seen at four, burgesses at one. Only to modern historians does the part seem
greater than the whole.

Whether under the barons or under the king, whether after
1258 or before it, the business of parliament remained
unchanged: in general it was consultation with the barons on
public affairs and the supervision of the work of administrative
departments and courts of law, particularly by advising on
problems arising therein: on this ground alone frequent parliaments were essential. We would forbear from speaking of
'petitions in parliament' under Henry III.[36] To settle this
point some twenty-six thousand petitions were examined
individually without a single one being found before 1272
which was addressed to the king or the king and his council
and which carried the endorsements common to parliamentary
petitions after 1272. There was as yet no general access to the
king in parliament. The barons in 1258 had arranged in parliament the means for righting wrongs and removing oppressions, but the form it took was to collect men's grievances locally and to try the plaints locally in tribunals the barons had
devised. And under Henry III it was the practice for ministers
and judges alone to refer matters to parliament for discussion.
There is no need—and, as we suggest below, little chance—to
list these matters: they come from the justiciar as he made his
tour through the country to investigate wrongdoings, from the

35. G. O. Sayles, 'Representation of Cities and Boroughs in 1268',
English Hist. Review, xl (1925), 583–85.
36. As does J. E. A. Jolliffe, 'Some Factors in the Beginnings of
Parliament', *Trans. Royal Hist. Soc.*, xxii (1940), 101–39. And it should
be observed that there was in fact no special relationship with parliament
that was peculiar to the exchequer itself, while loose and too often
meaningless language like 'the court of the capital justices', 'judges parliamentary in standing', 'legal councils', 'two kinds of parliament' (p. 113),
and 'parliament of barons' can only muddle and mislead.

king's bench, from the justices of the Jews.[37] They include the consideration of an assize of *novel disseisin* which seemed likely to stand in the way of recovering rights, lost 'between the battle of Evesham and the parliament of Winchester (September 1265), a time which was a time of war'; the legal problems concerning the Disinherited (that is, those who had lost their property in consequence of the civil war and sought to buy it back); the improvement in the administration of justice, as stated in the preamble to the Statute of Marlborough of 1267; the deliberation upon the conflicting evidence of juries from four hundreds of Northamptonshire; the entertainment of a strange case in 1269 where a robbery was openly admitted but it was claimed to have been done in time of war on the earl of Gloucester's instructions.[38]

The difficulty is to guess—and we can do no more than guess—the extent to which administrative and judicial questions were adjourned to parliament. And yet it seems impossible to suppose that such scattered and sparse notes as we have on the rolls of chancery and exchequer and on plea rolls represent the full volume of business of this kind. The little of which we have knowledge seems but a sample. It is quite clear that the rolls of chancery do not give at any time a complete picture of the work of chancery. Hundreds upon hundreds of documents were written and despatched without being enrolled if they were regarded as too trivial, too ephemeral, too routine to be worth recording. We know that at this time writs of summons were issued for parliaments which met at other times than the great festivals, but very few are enrolled.[39] We even have replies to writs of which there is no enrolment. Let us give an illustration. A man had risked hunting in the warren of Henry of Pembridge without the owner's permission, and on Henry's behalf the justiciar, Philip Basset, wrote to the chancellor, Walter of Merton, asking him to issue a writ, summoning the

37. Assize Rolls, no. 873, m. 6; no. 362, m. 8; no. 167, m. 10; no. 911, m. 6*d*; Curia Regis Roll, no. 192 (Trinity 1270), m. 15; Close Roll, no. 87, m. 17 (*Close Rolls, 1259–61*, p. 343).

38. Coram Rege Roll, no. 37 (Easter 1275), m. 32; Patent Roll, no. 84, m. 9*d* (*Cal. Patent Rolls, 1258–66*, p. 671–72); *Red Book of the Exchequer* (*Statutes of the Realm*, i.19ff.); Assize Rolls, no. 618, m. 17*d*; no. 42, m. 8*d*.

39. Richardson and Sayles, *Parliaments and Great Councils in Medieval England*, pp. 47–48.

offender to appear in parliament 'because in the uncertainty within the realm it is essential to protect as strongly as possible the privileges accorded by kings and to defend them so that an occasion for offending may be removed from those who desire to promote dissension'.[40] There is no reason to suppose that the writ was not issued in response to a request from such high authority, but it was certainly not enrolled. Unless a writ was in some way unusual, there was really no reason why the clerks should enrol it: the draft on the files would preserve all the necessary evidence for the short time it was required. Indeed, for no reason at all except sheer lack of diligence, much else might be left uncopied on the files. Nor can we suppose that the enrolling clerks in the exchequer were more punctilious than their brethren in the chancery or that the clerks of the law courts should allude to any private correspondence that caused actions to be transferred to parliament.

The point we must bring home is that enrolments are in no sense complete and not infrequently inaccurate. But even when we have assembled every surviving scrap of evidence, we have but a collection of fragments for the reign of Henry III. In the reign of his son, Edward I, though the volume of evidence is incomparably greater, it is but partial: for instance, we know little or nothing of what was done in the so-called Model Parliament of 1295. It is desirable, therefore, at the outset to impress upon the reader the limitations within which the early history of parliament must be written, especially in regard to those matters which did not seem to contemporaries to be of serious consequence. We can be reasonably confident that we can learn much—nearly everything of importance, perhaps—about legislation and finance. But minor matters, which represented the sober, less dramatic work of parliament, we are in danger of undervaluing simply because we are told so little about them. For many generations historians have looked upon parliament as a political institution where great causes were decided. We invite the reader to consider also the possibility that to contemporaries its importance was that of a supreme tribunal, a last resort, where minor, sometimes very small, matters might receive attention and justice be done not only to the

40. Ancient Correspondence, vol. vii, no. 211.

great but also to the humble. This will certainly be the main theme of the next chapter.

But before we leave the reign of Henry III we must say emphatically that there is not the slightest evidence that his parliaments before 1272 were essentially different in character from those of his son after 1272. Why should we suppose that the demise of the crown marked 'a new and very different stage in the history of parliament'? [41] Let us bring into the argument an unprinted document to which we attach high importance. It is plain that after Evesham Henry III had learned no prudence in finance. His council found it necessary in October 1269 [42] to have all his grants of fees, other than to those actually in his service, annulled. Yet by the autumn of 1270 the treasury was empty, creditors could not be paid, and no lender, Christian or Jew, would make further advances to so irresponsible a borrower. Eventually, in 1272, revenues were required to be paid direct into the treasury and not to be intercepted by the king before they got there.[43] The wheel had come full circle since 1258, when the reformers had had to make the same arrangements. Many did not regard the Lord Edward, his son, as more scrupulous or trustworthy or competent, and it is worth pondering the fact that, though he had been lord of Ireland since 1254 and drew a major part of his income therefrom, no interest in administration had ever manifested itself in him to induce him to set foot in that country. Certainly he saw no reason why he should not leave England in August 1270 on a crusade and remain absent for four years, even after his father's death in November 1272. In these sorry circumstances it was fortunate that the responsibilities of government rested with a most talented group of men in the king's service who knew the problems and somehow kept the country in working order. Now, Edward I had intended to hold

---

41. R. F. Treharne, *op. cit.*, p. 590. In similar vein the author thinks that the word 'parliament' was used 'in an unconsidered and haphazard fashion' before 1258 (p. 601), 'changed from an occasion into an institution' between 1258 and 1265 (p. 608), and lapsed again after 1265 into being 'once more an occasion rather than an institution' (p. 609). This 'stop-go-stop' procedure is flatly contradicted by the evidence.

42. *Cal. Patent Rolls*, 1266–72, p. 326.

43. K. R. Memoranda Roll, no. 47 (56–57 Henry III), m. 2d.

the first parliament of his reign on 16 February 1275, but in
the event he adjourned it until 22 April (the Morrow of the
Close, i.e., Octave of Easter). Nevertheless there was a meeting of the king's council in February, and it has left us the
minutes of its decisions, made apparently over several days.[44]
One minute gives us the names of some of those present.
They include Walter Giffard, former chancellor (1265), archbishop of York, and regent; Robert Burnell, bishop-elect of
Bath and Wells and chancellor (1274–92); Master Thomas
de Cantilupe, doctor of canon law, former chancellor (1264)
and bishop of Hereford (1275–82); Stephen of Penchester,
warden of the Cinque Ports; Ralph Hengham, chief justice of
the king's bench (1274–89); Master Roger of Seyton, chief
justice of the common bench (1274); Robert Neville, Walter
of Helion, Nicholas of Stapleton, Roger of Leicester, who were
all royal justices. Among other things these men, high in government service, were considering the arrangements to be
made for the forthcoming Easter parliament and drawing up
agenda for its consideration. All of them had seen parliament
at work under Henry III and played a prominent part therein
and there would have been no reason why the parliament-
to-be should not be in the same mould as the parliaments
they had intimately known in the past. What kind of parliament, then, was in the minds of these members of the king's
council and what in their opinion was the business they expected it to do? Having settled the form in which the writs
of summons were to be couched and the form of writs to be
issued in connexion with a proposed new tax on wool, they
considered the matters brought before them. Some they could
answer outright; others had to be deferred to parliament. This
glimpse of the council at work is unique and therefore we
think it well to cite some of its minutes.

> The earl de Ferrers is given a day to appear at a Fortnight
> after Easter in the parliament etc. concerning the demands upon
> his manor of Chartley.
> Concerning the prisoners taken within the liberty of the
> abbot of Bury St. Edmunds, who are to be handed over to the
> sheriff of Northamptonshire etc. Otherwise let another day be

44. Exchequer Miscellanea, file 2, no. 39. This document incorporates
the decisions of the king on the treatment of his brother, Edmund, a
subject which is itself of considerable interest.

given on the Morrow of the Close of Easter [45] for the exhibition of his charters whereby he claims to have such prisoners in his custody.

Concerning the business of the Master of the Temple etc.: he is given a day to appear at a Fortnight after Easter etc. and in the meantime let him have a respite from distraints etc.

William Belet is given a day to appear at a Fortnight after Easter etc. and he shall show his charter concerning strengthening his house at Marham.

Let the record of the outlawry of Walter de Baskerville be sent before the king at a Fortnight after Easter.

Concerning the captives imprisoned in the time of King Henry: let the matter be postponed until a Fortnight after Easter etc.

Let the park of Potterspury [Northamptonshire] be restored to John fitz John until parliament etc. And the wood in Wiltshire.

The attorney of Arnald du Bois is given a postponement with regard to the customs of Haversham, until parliament.

Let the abbot of Darnhall and the men of Memwich be given a day to appear, with regard to the exaction of toll etc., in the Octave of Easter, namely, in parliament.[46]

Let Roger of Clifford, the justice of the Forest, be written to so that he can inform the king in his parliament for what reason Thomas de Kenum was amerced before him etc. And meanwhile distraint is to cease etc.

We trust we have not wearied the reader with these humdrum details of business deferred for consideration in parliament. Are these men, who knew only the parliaments of Henry III, thinking in terms primarily of a 'political assembly' or primarily of a tribunal established to deal with the problems of government as they emerged in departments and courts of law? In short, what weight do we attribute to the evidence of men on the spot?

45. I.e., 22 April, the day for which parliament was summoned.
46. The last three words seem to be added in a different hand. Early in 1274 the earl of Cornwall had asked the chancellor to see that certain wrongdoers came in person 'before the council or nobles of England in the next parliament at London' (Ancient Correspondence, vol. vii, no. 82). This is the earliest reference to parliament under Edward I known to us, and it too assumes that parliament is there for administering justice and even seems to suppose that it might be held in the king's absence.

5. The Parliaments
of Edward I:
The Age of Bureaucracy

In the thirteenth century Englishmen could hardly fail to observe the dispensation of justice all around them. The courts of ecclesiastical jurisdiction held by bishops and archdeacons apart, they knew the hall-moots with their enforcement of by-laws, the courts for manorial tenants, the borough courts and market courts with the special rules, known as the Law Merchant, the courts held every three weeks in the divisions of a shire called 'hundreds', the monthly or six-weekly sessions of the shire court itself. And beside these local jurisdictions they saw in their midst the agencies of the central government: the occasional courts of the justices in eyre, the innumerable courts of special commission to hear assizes or to try prisoners in the gaols or to punish crime and even investigate official misconduct. And at headquarters sat the three courts of common law: king's bench, common bench, and exchequer of pleas. Nothing reveals more vividly the extent of law and its increasing sophistication than the growth of the legal profession with its practitioners firmly based in the counties as well as in Westminster and with *Glanville*, Bracton, *Fleta*, and a goodly collection of smaller manuals for their use. The city of London by 1280 had already drawn up regulations to control the activities of the lawyers within its walls. The busy legal system was interconnected, and at its head was the court above all other courts, what came to be known as the high court of parliament.

It is self-evident that by the time Edward I became king

parliament was an institution with a precise meaning for government ministers and judges, for civil servants, for lawyers and their clients, for all whose affairs required them to have a care for technicalities. When departments and courts adjourned business before them simply 'to the next parliament', we cannot imagine that interested parties were in a complete quandary about what this meant and did not know where or when to put in an appearance. Indeed, we can hold in our hands the very letters which summoned a man to come 'to the next parliament' without any further details, and parliament must have meant for him a meeting of a definite kind at a definite time at a definite place, for such letters had to be obeyed. This being so, it is not difficult to construct a list of parliaments under Edward I: out of nearly fifty parliaments convened in 1275–1307, only three cause us to hesitate because evidence is either lacking or is confused.[1] It seems to have been decided at the first parliament at Easter 1275 that there should be two parliaments a year, one after Easter and the other after Michaelmas—in other words, every spring and every autumn [2]—and this practice was as well known to the papal curia at Rome and the French court at Paris as it was at home. Occasionally an additional parliament might be intercalated, as at Midsummer 1278 at Gloucester. But this ordered arrangement was inevitably disrupted in the stress of special circumstances, usually war in Wales or Gascony or Scotland, or the king's long absence from his kingdom in 1286–89. Particularly after 1293, when the Easter and Michaelmas parliaments were held as usual, the incidence of parliaments became irregular and they had to be convoked when and where it was most convenient.[3]

The king was almost invariably present in person, though he might appoint commissioners to open proceedings in preparation for his arrival. Very rarely did he authorise others to take his place right through the session, as in 1297 when he was busy in Flanders and appointed his son to deputise for him. So long as parliament met at regular times and at Westminster

1. For example, for a detailed examination of the conflicting evidence concerning the assembly in May 1306 see Richardson and Sayles, *Parliaments and Great Councils*, pp. 24–30.
2. Already on 16 May 1275 it was known that the next parliament would be at Michaelmas (Ancient Correspondence, vol. xiv, no. 53).
3. Cf. *Mirror of Justices*, pp. 155f.: 'It is an abuse that, whereas parliaments ought to be held twice a year, they are now held but rarely.'

or London—and only a fifth of his parliaments met anywhere
else—it was needless to send writs of summons to those normally expected to attend,[4] and we certainly have no record of
them. But if the king desired an especially large attendance,
or if a parliament was to meet away from London, as at Shrews-
bury or Winchester or York, or if it were to assemble at an
unusual time, then it was necessary to give advance warning.
This took the form of writs of summons to those who were
required to be there, but they were far from being the only
ones to whom a meeting of parliament was of consequence.
As we shall see, people in every part of England were concerned, and there was no difficulty in acquiring information, for
England was a much governed and busy country with a
remarkable criss-cross of messengers, professional messengers,
travelling regularly between London—or where the court,
chancery, and king's bench happened to be—and the local
regions.

The king's council, meeting in augmented session in parliament, embraced in its composition only two elements that
were regarded as essential, and we may conveniently label them
as 'aristocratic' and 'ministerial'. The aristocratic members were
earls and barons, bishops and abbots. The king's feudatories
like the earls and barons were under a solemn obligation to
serve the king not only with their arms but with their counsel,
not only in his wars but in his parliaments. The barons claimed
that they were the natural guardians of the common good and
consequently a restraint upon the power of monarchy. There
was no stereotyped list of those who must attend: in 1295
seven earls and forty-one barons were summoned; in 1305 nine
earls and ninety-four barons. Discrepancy as wide as this was
seen for many years and is quite understandable when so much
depended on the king's will, the caprice of chancery, the kind
of business to be transacted, the length of time at the government's disposal. The fantastic theory that held good for so
long in law, that a summons by writ to parliament under Edward I established an hereditary right to be summoned there-

4. In 1281 the justices in eyre in Devon had to ask the chancellor
if they all ought to come to parliament: if so, they could not fit an eyre
in Cornwall in between Easter and parliament (Ancient Correspondence,
vol. xxiv, no. 74: printed Sayles, *King's Bench*, i. pp. cxlii f.).

after, has been killed by ridicule, so little did this fiction fit the facts, and nineteenth-century democracy, which saw every reason to vindicate the myths of its own origins, saw no reason to come to the aid of the peers. The conception of peerage and its association with a small group of aristocrats was the result of a political upheaval under Edward II,[5] and only by slow steps did it later become accepted doctrine. We must remember that there were many councils attended by feudatories and ministers that were not necessarily parliaments, for the king might require his council to be afforced at any time to deal with special problems. Business, though appropriate to parliament, could not always conveniently wait for its assembly.

The bishops had a position in parliament because most of them held their temporalities, their secular property, 'by barony', that is, by tenure-in-chief of the king, and must attend.[6] But the bishops were never in any meaningful sense in a feudal relation with the Crown, and any effort to assimilate bishops with barons could not obliterate the hard fact that bishops always had a dual loyalty, to the pope as well as to the king. As for abbots and priors, there was no restriction on the king's prerogative to order members of the higher clergy other than bishops to come to parliament, whether or not they had 'tenure by barony'. But there was no consistent practice: not all abbots or all priors were summoned, though on occasion, a large number attended and the list might, indeed, include abbesses.[7] The motive for their summons was, above all, financial, and in time many of them sought to evade on one ground or other the obligation to attend. We may perhaps tell the end of the story here, especially because it shows so well the casual nature of the composition of parliament. At the parliament at York at Easter 1319 the abbot of Northampton, while agreeing 'that all people in the kingdom, no matter from whom or how they hold their lands, must come at the king's summons', went on to demur that neither he nor any of his predecessors had ever previously been summoned; 'to deal with this petition the

5. See below, pp. 100–101.
6. The bishops of Rochester and Carlisle did not hold 'by barony', though they obeyed summons to attend parliament. In any case 'barony' was never a strictly legal or administrative term.
7. In May 1306; see below, p. 139.

chancellor decided, in agreement with his chancery council, that the abbot's name was to be erased from the chancery register, and thus in the sight of many onlookers the abbot was excused. But because the abbot and his successors might on another occasion be accidentally put on the roll', he had what was done set down in writing 'by way of evidence'.[8] The determination to dodge attendance remained. For example, the abbot of Thornton claimed that his predecessors had not been at the king's parliaments and councils before 1311–12 and they were afterwards 'summoned not continuously but occasionally'. But now they were being harassed by having to be present frequently and quite contrary to what was customary. The abbots of Thornton were discharged from any further obligation, 'provided they agreed to send clerical proctors to these parliaments and councils and contributed to their expenses in the usual way'.[9] Thus the abbots and priors summoned to parliament, who had numbered eighty-five in 1305, had been reduced to twenty-seven by the end of Edward III's reign, and not all even of these troubled to attend. The general tendency was to regard the heads of only the important religious houses as being, with the bishops, 'spiritual peers', and these prelates were absorbed without difficulty in the 'house of lords'.

The second essential element in the king's council in parliament we have comprehensively termed 'ministerial': it reached the height of its influence under Edward I and never again will England be so effectively controlled by it. No section of society was immune from its investigations in the interests of the Crown. It is impossible here to recount its activities, for we would then be engaged with the whole study of government, and we can but provide a few graphic illustrations. Exchequer officials on their own initiative, in order to secure more revenue, altered the terms of an ordinance.[10] The judges drafted legislation: 'Do not gloss the statute', said Chief Jus-

8. *Parl. Writs*, ii.199f. An abbot of Northampton had been summoned to Simon de Montfort's parliament of 1265, but this had apparently made no lasting impression.

9. King's Remembrancer's Memoranda Roll, no. 121 (19 Edward III), m. 130*d*. The abbots of Thornton had been summoned twice under Edward I, in 1295 and 1299 (*Parl. Writs*, i.38, 78).

10. G. O. Sayles, 'The Seizure of Wool at Easter 1297', *English Hist. Review*, lxvii (1952), 543–47.

tice Hengham in 1305, 'we understand it better than you do, for we made it'; [11] and they acted as legal consultants to all who could pay an appropriate fee.[12] The chancery clerks constructed new forms of writs to meet the rapidly expanding requirements of law and administration,[13] and acted as proctors in parliament for absent prelates and nobles. The story has still to be told of the nepotism whereby the king's clerks intruded their relatives into every branch of the law courts and the administration and how their monopoly of government posts was not only lucrative to their own families but founded firm and valuable traditions of public service.[14]

Sometimes the king found it convenient to discuss affairs, almost always relating to taxation, in parliament with elected representatives of the lower clergy, the shires, and the boroughs, but the occasions were infrequent. All that concerns us here is to note that their presence was not essential to parliament, which was just as omnicompetent whether they were there or not. Arguments to the contrary would not have amused Edward I, if indeed he could have understood them.

We turn now from the composition of parliament to its functions, a far more important matter for consideration. The history of parliament is first and foremost the history of a particular contrivance of government. As the conditions of society change, adjustments have to be made to fit them. There is a great deal of experimentation, and some of the experiments are not very wise and come to be discarded, like summoning the lower clergy to parliament. And business brought to parliament may not retain its original significance and may diminish or

11. *Year Book, 33–35 Edward I,* p. 82. For a list of those, mainly judges, who devised the Statute of Escheators in 1301, see Chancery, Parliament and Council Proceedings, file 3, no. 1, with which cf. *Statutes of the Realm,* i.142.

12. G. O. Sayles, 'Medieval Judges as Legal Consultants', *Law Quarterly Review,* lvi (1940), 247–54.

13. Elsa de Haas and G. D. G. Hall, *Early Registers of Writs.* The writs that had to be formulated in accordance with new statutes furnish a simple illustration. Cf. Ancient Correspondence, vol. xxii, no. 179: the earl of Cornwall, when writing to Robert Burnell, the chancellor, 'requested that you should be so good as to write to the justices by a letter from the king or at least by a letter from you if we cannot have a letter from the king'.

14. Sayles, *King's Bench,* i. p. cxliv, vi. p. xxxvi, vii. p. xvi.

even vanish. We shall never understand parliament if we do not
remember that it was always dynamic, never static.

We have already pointed out that the dispensation of justice had always formed part of the work of parliament. Judicial questions had before 1272 come before it by reference
from ministers, judges, and other government officials and,
apart from a few persons of exalted rank, it could not be
approached direct. Not until 1275 or very shortly afterwards
does parliament come within range of the people at large by
way of straight petition. This deliberate magnification of the
judicial work parliament was required to undertake merits a
somewhat detailed discussion, for though we do not know the
master mind and the precise reasons behind it all, we can
place it against its background and free ourselves from the
guess-work which attributed to the clergy the major responsibility for 'moulding the petitionary technique'.[15]

In and before Henry III's reign the redress of wrong might
be sought by two different methods of procedure, either by
writ or by bill. A writ to originate an action at law could be
obtained only in the chancery, wherever it chanced to be in
attendance on the king, and at a price. Its essence was its
formalism: the litigant had to be absolutely sure that the writ
he obtained fitted his case and was properly worded, otherwise it spelt disaster for him in the courts. Bills stood out in
sharp contrast. They were written on odds and ends of parchment; they were almost invariably, not in Latin like the writs,
but in French; they rarely bore a date; apparently no fee was
charged before they could be presented. Their main characteristic therefore was their informality, being addressed direct
to the justices, couched in no right form of words, telling a
story of how a wrong had been committed, ending often with
a fervent prayer that justice should be done. Now, the system
of writs (though not, of course, writs themselves) came into
operation only with the reform policy of Henry II. The author of *Glanville*, that is, the late twelfth-century treatise on
legal procedure, was interested in it alone as the legal novelty
of his day. Bracton six decades later could declare that 'no

15. H. M. Cam, 'Theory and Practice of Representation in Medieval
England', *History*, xxxviii (1953), 17. It should be observed that much
was already known by then about procedure without writ.

man may bring an action without a writ, for the other party will not be bound to answer without one', and he had very little to say about bills.[16] He was concerned almost exclusively with land law and pleas of the Crown. It follows that we obtain from him a somewhat lopsided view of the business of the courts of law, for he did not realise that the bill, which he evidently regarded as a relic of a departed age, a legal curiosity, was on the brink of a tremendous development which was to cause litigation by writ to be less common than litigation by bill.[17] For from times immemorial it had always been recognised that anyone with a grievance ought to have access to the king as the fountain of justice or to his representative in order to obtain redress. The records we now have of action by bill do not predate the so-called Inquest of Sheriffs in 1170 but a chain of evidence exists thereafter throughout the Middle Ages. It is true that for nearly a hundred years after 1170 the practice of hearing bills was not very extensive: not many found their way before the central courts and most were heard in the eyre courts.[18] But there was much wrongdoing which was not being redressed by the use of writs, especially because the conservative circles of the barons viewed the issue of new writs with suspicion as a danger to their own privileged position.[19] The discontent grew so much under Henry III that in 1258 the reforming barons decreed that the office of justiciar should be revived and that he should be given the duty of hearing complaints made by bill throughout the land. Inevitably the work proved too heavy for him alone, and in the autumn of 1259 tribunals of special commissioners were established, each to work within a prescribed circuit. We see no new ideas but the deliberate exploitation of an old and well-known procedure. What the barons sought to do had no chance to work itself out. Still, all over England men had been encouraged to present their bills and to expect redress: not new

16. He does refer to action by bill but only to emphasise the rule that, except with the defendant's consent, an action touching freehold must begin with a writ (*De Legibus*, fols. 112, 154*b*, 413*b*).

17. The exception was the court of common pleas, the home of freehold actions, which apparently admitted no bills.

18. See generally Richardson and Sayles, *Procedure without Writ.*

19. Curia Regis Rolls, nos. 116A, m. 11*d*, 120, m. 18, 133, m. 9: printed Sayles, *King's Bench*, ii. pp. cxxxviii, cxxxix, clvi.

remedies for new wrongs but the righting of wrongs which would never have been righted if the use of writs had been insisted upon. The triumph of the king did nothing to appease the pent-up resentment, especially against official misconduct, of people in general. We must not be misled into thinking in terms of a homogeneous 'community of England'. There was little kinship of thought between the aristocracy and their social inferiors, that struggling mass of all sorts and conditions of men who were divided from them not only by interests but often by language and possessed at best of only the most rudimentary political conceptions. The bond of unity was a universal distrust of the king that explains the appeal of Simon de Montfort alike to the high-born and to the lowly in town and countryside and the veneration sixty years later of the unworthy Thomas of Lancaster. This distrust springs now from one cause, now from another, and if it is stilled from time to time it is always ready to emerge: indeed, the mistrust of monarchy is as significant in the history of the English constitution as the equally widespread and deep-seated mistrust of the papacy was in the history of the medieval Church. Edward I when he was simply the Lord Edward had aroused against himself the most bitter and forthright criticism from his contemporaries,[20] and his subjects must have had misgivings as he dallied for months in France before returning to his new kingdom. Fortunately he had wise and prudent men to advise him and he authorised at once farreaching measures of reform. It may have been—we can but conjecture—part and parcel of them that all who felt themselves aggrieved should be allowed to present bills, that is petitions, in parliament and ask for relief. It may indeed have been intended as a stop-gap arrangement until a general eyre was authorised in 1278: if there was no opportunity for bills to be presented to the king's representatives in the local districts under a government-sponsored scheme, then they might at least be presented to the king at headquarters at the initiative of the petitioners themselves. It seems to have been a wise stroke of policy, for the very essence of government is the settling of disputes at all levels. This new twist to an old pro-

20. *The Song of Lewes*, ed. C. L. Kingsford.

cedure was immediately and highly popular. The redress of individual grievances, whether of barons or tin-miners, lordly prelates or humble clerks, on every conceivable subject became in the eyes of the people at large the dominant purpose of parliament. If we were to subtract the record of judicial business from the parliament rolls of Edward I's reign, we should be left with little else.[21]

Strictly speaking, we should not use the term English parliament but the king's parliament of England. For parliament in England was never less specifically national than under Edward I, who cared at least as much for his dominions overseas as at home. Gascon and Irish affairs had already come to the parliaments of Henry III and now, with the inception of the new petitory procedure, a spate of petitions arrived from Edward I's possessions abroad, to be swollen with petitions from Scotland when he claimed to be the suzerain of that kingdom. Indeed, so great was the total volume that it soon became urgent to classify the petitions according to their country of origin and allot them to separate tribunals for expedition, that is for Ireland, for Gascony[22] and the Channel Isles, for Scotland.

But petitions from England by itself became well-nigh un-

21. The terms 'bill' and 'petition' were interchangeable and imply no differences. Both express a plaint, a complaint, a *querela*. But it became the common custom to speak of a 'petition' to parliament until the fifteenth century, by which time we begin to hear of 'public bills' and 'private bills'. A petition as a means of originating an action is now known only in the Divorce Court, while the other kind of petition known to the twentieth century, the 'petition of right' against the Crown, was abolished in 1948.

22. The hearing of Gascon petitions was not a task quite comparable with that of hearing petitions from other lands of the king's obedience, for appeals from Gascony on points of law had a habit of going to the *parlement* of Paris. The English king sought in various ways to discourage appeals to his French overlord: sometimes through the renunciation of this right by the parties (Chancery Miscellanea 25/4/6: a notarial act of 1320–21), mostly by endeavouring to facilitate the hearing and final adjudication of appeals in Gascony itself (Ancient Correspondence, vol. xxxiii, no. 20). Still, there was no effective way of preventing appeals to Paris until after the outbreak of the Hundred Years' War. We should perhaps observe that legal procedure in Gascony was based on that of the kingdom of France and differed as much from the procedure of the English courts as Gascon law and custom differed from the English common law.

manageable, running as they did in some parliaments into their hundreds. The procedure for coping with them had to be constantly adjusted, and we have the record of at least two sets of new regulations. In 1280 it was decided that after the petitions had been sorted out, they should first be sent to the departments and courts they concerned—the chancery, the exchequer, the justices of the common law courts, the justices of the Jewry—and only those that could not be disposed of there were to be transmitted to the king and council. The balance of parliamentary business had been badly upset, for only 'thus can the king and his council attend to the great affairs of his kingdom and of his lands abroad without being burdened with other matters'.[23] An ordinance of 1293 made similar arrangements for petitions.[24] But these were apparently temporary expedients and did not represent the normal procedure. By 1305 it had become standardised. Before parliament assembled, a proclamation was made that petitions were to be written out and handed in by a specified day to government clerks, styled the receivers of petitions. These made a preliminary weeding-out, rejecting those which in their opinion should not have been brought to parliament: some still survive which must have come from the mentally disordered. The rest they arranged in bundles according to the country from which they originated and passed them to the appropriate tribunals of auditors of petitions, to whom they themselves then acted as clerks, looking after the files of petitions—answered, unanswered, pending—and supervising their enrolment. The auditors dealt with most of the petitions before them out of hand: the well-known parliament roll of 1305, edited by Maitland,[25] is, in fact, not one roll but separate rolls of proceedings before three tribunals of auditors. But they sent difficult cases to a committee of the council, and it might in its wisdom decide that some of them ought to be discussed before the whole of the king's council; cases of intimate concern to the king they

23. Close Roll, no. 85, m. 6*d* (schedule): printed Ehrlich, *Proceedings against the Crown*, p. 235.
24. Close Roll, no. 110, m. 7 (schedule): printed Ehrlich, *op. cit.*, p. 90.
25. *Memoranda de Parliamento.*

reserved for his personal decision.[26] That the English parliament today should do its hardest, if not its most dramatic, work in committee and not on the floor of the House is nothing new: this is how it worked some seven hundred years ago. How long decisions took to reach, how much argument lay behind them, why the petitions had to come to parliament at all: these are questions to which we rarely have an answer.[27] But the work of tribunals, committees, council was far too heavy to allow lengthy discussions to take place or many final judgements to be made: instead the petitioners were directed to the right place, be it a department, a court, or specially appointed commissioners, and authority was given for justice to be done there. If more petitions were presented than could be handled during the session of parliament, it was not unknown for a committee to be appointed to hear the disappointed petitioners after parliament had ended.

Petitions apart, problems of law and administration continued to be referred to parliament by those responsible for the governance of the realm and, as their work expanded and became more complex, it resulted in a constantly increasing burden upon parliament. For example, a considerable body of work came in the form of returns to inquests, that is, answers to government inquiries upon a multitude of matters concerning administration. There are signs that a special committee was once appointed to deal with such business. In 1285 the clerks of chancery were required 'to write down the cases in which they cannot agree and report them to the next parliament';[28] only in parliament could the errors of the king's bench be reviewed and amended.

It is therefore not surprising that from the beginning of Edward I's reign the ordering of parliamentary business be-

26. The procedure described is made plain by successive instructions endorsed on petitions. Harl. MS. 6806, fols. 353–60, gives abstracts in English of more than fifty petitions in the autumn parliament of 1305, apparently those that went before the council.

27. For the discussions before the king's council in parliament in 1292 which established the so-called Statute of Waste, see *Rot. Parl.*, i. 79; for the discussions on a petition, see Sayles, *King's Bench*, ii. pp. cxxvi, cxl f.

28. Statute of Westminster II, c. 24 (*Statutes of the Realm*, i.83f.)

fore, during, and after its sessions had to be placed under expert supervision. The records are replete with references to the activities of the first clerk of the council, John Kirkby, a chancery clerk who was destined to be treasurer in 1284 and to die as the bishop of Ely in 1290. No document known to us gives him that title but there is not the slightest doubt that he is doing the work associated with that office and, in particular, during parliament. Numerous letters were sent to him, requesting him to have this or that business brought to parliament. He received apologies for absence. One petition was even addressed: 'To the council of our lord the king and especially to John Kirkby, bishop of Ely'.[29] He was succeeded in 1290 by Gilbert Rothbury, a lawyer, who was made a justice of the king's bench in 1295. He was unequivocally styled 'clerk of the council' [30] and served it until his elevation to the bench. He was also the clerk of parliament and continued to act as such until the end of the reign and maybe a few years later. With him we get the first of the surviving series of parliament rolls, beginning with the Hilary parliament of 1290. It should be said that Rothbury saw no reason to keep his duties as clerk of the council out of parliament rigidly separate from his duties as clerk of the council in parliament, and the so-called rolls of parliament reveal him acting in both capacities. Certainly a set of parliament rolls from 1290 onwards was written at his behest and was in his official custody.

It is impossible here to give in detail the qualifications of the receivers and the auditors of petitions: the former were drawn from the king's clerks employed in chancery, exchequer, or wardrobe; the latter were mainly ministers, judges, or prominent lawyers. A few of the minor barons and knights may be called to assist the auditors, but the great nobles were seldom employed in work for which they had little qualification and less interest. The business of parliament was in the hands of trained experts and no one can read the precise, succinct, and lucid endorsements of the petitions without appreciating the professional competence responsible for them.

As we have already said, we do not think that contemporaries could have had the slightest difficulty in distinguishing

29. Ancient Petition, no. 1589.
30. 'clericus consilii', not 'clericus de consilio'.

between parliaments and other assemblies. To modern eyes the picture is blurred because the king possessed and exercised the right to discuss matters of state elsewhere than in parliament and he could do justice when and where he pleased. Petitions were delivered to him and his council at any time and many of the documents now termed 'Ancient Petitions' were certainly not presented in parliament. But those who petitioned outside parliament had no acknowledged right to petition and no acknowledged right to be answered. The position with regard to parliament was quite different. There and there only the king officially appointed receivers and auditors and he indisputably thereby gave his subjects an opportunity to petition, an opportunity that was provided specifically in parliament. By implication he gave them also an expectation that they would be answered, for every effort was made to that end. Constant repetition, constant usage, created a recognisable right. It is true that the right was a qualified right and, indeed, an unenforceable right, for the king might not choose to summon a parliament. We know, however, that the conventions of the English constitution today, though not enforceable in the courts, are almost as important as statute law or custom which is enforceable. So it was in the Middle Ages. The failure to receive petitions in parliament aroused resentment.[31] At no other assembly, however afforced in composition, however important its business, was the right to present petitions acknowledged by any preparations for the implementation of that right. Therein lies the difference which makes all the difference, and contemporaries knew it well. The argument that the petitioners asked for 'grace' and not for justice [32] does not explain the facts. To ask for 'grace' was frequently no more than to request the king to waive the royal prerogative and thus allow the practices of the common law to become operative.[33] What the petitioner obtained was an ordinary writ, based on a normal and standard formula. Some petitions, of course, required administrative rather than judicial action, and some sought gifts and rewards, but the overwhelming majority

31. See below, pp. 109–10.
32. Sir Goronwy Edwards, 'Historians and the Medieval English Parliament' (1960), p. 16.
33. Sayles, *King's Bench*, v. pp. lxxxi–lxxxviii.

pleaded for justice. For more than fifty years parliament was
valued by the people at large because it provided them with
a chance, maybe their only chance, to get redress for their
wrongs, often inflicted upon them by those who served the
king and against whom there could be no action by writ in the
ordinary courts of law.

Because parliament was a court of law it was surrounded
during its sessions by a special sanctity, out of which was to
evolve the privileges of parliament. So majestic was this sanctity that the ordinary processes of law could not prevail against
it and, indeed, if they were used they became an offence.[34]
Members of the king's council, clerks employed in parliament,
were immune from arrest and from distraint, no citations to
appear in other courts could be served while parliament was
in session; those who attended parliament were specially pro-
tected in coming, staying, and departing, and to injure any of
their servants back home while they themselves were 'in the
king's service at his parliament at Westminster' was particularly heinous. To appear with arms or to brawl in parliament
was strictly forbidden. It was with justification that Westminster was regarded at the time as 'the freest place in England'.[35]

It may seem that we have unduly neglected the 'showy
side' of politics, the great disputes and great catastrophes.[36]
For parliaments were summoned by the king so that 'the
state of the realm' or 'the common affairs of the king and the
kingdom' could be considered: questions of war and peace,
the framing of legislation, the grant of taxation, the progress of
diplomacy. In modern parlance we might comprehensively
speak of 'public affairs' or even 'high politics', and these were
always prominent in the business of the king's parliament.[37]
But it was not essential that they should be dealt with in
parliament and only in parliament, for they were often discussed in special and non-parliamentary assemblies. Even in
parliament they could not have engrossed much of the time of
a session which might last for months on end: in 1285 from

34. *Ibid.*, i.45.
35. Ryley, *Placita*, pp. 604f.
36. Maitland, 'The Materials for English Legal History', in *Collected
Papers*, ii.7.
37. For an analysis, set forth in 1934, of what was done in parliament, see Richardson and Sayles, *Rotuli Parliamentorum Inediti*, p. viii.

4 May to 4 June, in 1290 from 22 April to 15 July, in 1307 from
20 January to 19 March.[38] The daily business of parliament
is the dispensation of justice, the patient hearing of large numbers of petitions; it is not made up of great monuments of
legislation or dramatic disputes over taxation. Nevertheless
these two subjects came by the fifteenth century to be recognised as exclusive to parliament, and we should say something
more about them.

The reign of Edward I, especially the first half, was a
period of legislation, the like of which had not been seen since
before the Norman Conquest and would not be seen again
until the Long Parliament of the Reformation in 1529. Before
1066 the English kings had been notable as lawgivers, and their
legislation took a form which had no counterpart in England
before the thirteenth century.[39] For since Cnut (1016–35)
there had been no legislation on the grand scale, nothing comparable to set beside his laws. It is true that we can recover
something of the legislation of the Norman and Angevin kings
as reflected in the forms of action at law they authorised, forms
which bore the name 'assize'—the grand assize and the posses-
sory assizes. But no one sought to collect these laws, no one
bothered to find out the precise text. This casual attitude to
royal legislation persisted until the 1230s when, as we have
seen, apparently for the first time, chancery clerks began to
put together from the files the principal pieces of legislation [40]
and to inform the chroniclers of Burton Abbey and St. Albans
of the decisions made at great councils or parliaments, as they
were then beginning to be termed. It was realised that on occasion, however infrequent, the king would, with the advice of
his magnates, correct existing law and even make new law and
that the changes ought to be recorded and circulated. A new
attitude of mind had appeared before the parliament of Oxford

38. In 1281 justices of eyre envisaged a serious interruption in their
work if they were all required to return to Westminster 'on account of
the long stay in parliament' (Sayles, *King's Bench*, i. pp. cxlii f.).

39. This discussion is based on Richardson and Sayles, *The Early
Statutes; Governance of Mediaeval England; Law and Legislation.*

40. E.g., the so-called Statute of Merton (above, p. 40). Some of
the legislation promulgated in the parliament of 1237 was widely enough
known for a litigant to plead its provisions in court in 1239 (Sayles,
King's Bench, ii.p. cxxxix). The Statute of Merton is the first item on
the existing statute roll.

in 1258 deliberately undertook to amend the laws. The Provisions of Westminster of 1259 and the Statute of Marlborough of 1267 foreshadowed the remarkable legislative activity which has earned Edward I the title (somewhat misconceived) of the English Justinian. By the end of the century the idea of enacted law was familiar, for it was cited in court very speedily after it was passed and the author of *Fleta* brought Bracton's treatise up to date by incorporating the legislative changes under Edward I.

There was no idea that only in parliament could legislation be enacted, that popular representatives must be consulted about it, or that, when made, it was sacrosanct. The king had the right to review and alter statutes if they conflicted in his opinion with the public welfare or with his royal prerogatives: the Statute of Gloucester of 1278 was later supplemented by the king simply on the advice of his justices; the legislation passed in 1305 was not enforced until 1307. The judges did not regard statute law as immutable, but as part of the common law they felt free in their wisdom to interpret: there was no great gulf fixed between legislative authority and judicial authority. Nevertheless men's conceptions of the functions of parliament were bound to be affected when they saw statutes being based on their individual petitions [41] and revealed as an expression of justice. By 1327 the connexion between parliament and legislation had been firmly made.

The need for taxation provided the motive for sometimes summoning to parliament representatives from the lower classes of society. This was the unanimous conclusion of seventeenth-century scholars, and other explanations put forward later have failed to square with the evidence. It is common to think solely in terms of the representatives of shires and boroughs and to ignore the representatives of the lower clergy because in time, though they never ceased to be summoned, they ceased to attend. Yet they were all in like case and, if we would understand the early history of the 'commons', the knights and burgesses, in parliament, we would do well not to ignore the lower clergy in parliament.

The lower clergy were summoned to parliament for the

41. G. O. Sayles, 'The Sources of Two Revisions of the Statute of Gloucester, 1278', *English Hist. Review*, lii (1937), 467–74.

first time at Easter 1254, and this was also the first time that knights of the shire appeared there. The reason for their attendance was to rescue the king from the desperate financial straits in which his foreign policy had placed him. The lower clergy were, as was the custom of the time, vested with plenary powers to speak on behalf of those they represented, and their grant of a tenth was accompanied by a statement of grievances it was hoped the king would amend. This *quid pro quo*, the tie between subsidy and redress, was so inevitable and natural a process in bargaining that common sense might suggest that there is little profit in seeking to prove that the clergy taught the apparently ignorant laity how it was done. After 1254 demands for subsidies from the clergy were placed before the provincial councils (or convocations) of Canterbury and York and it was not until 1283 that the lower clergy were required to be present, again in the company of knights of the shire and burgesses, at two councils, one at York for the north and one at Northampton for the south, to make the king a grant.[42] In 1295 the writ summoning the bishops to parliament in November contained a clause requiring (*praemunientes*) of them that they were to arrange for two proctors to attend on behalf of each diocese, and the reason for their presence was again avowedly financial. Afterwards representatives of the lower clergy came intermittently: they were at the parliaments of 1296, 1300, 1305, and 1307 but not at a dozen or so parliaments convened between 1295 and 1307. After 1307

42. Historians are somewhat baffled by the evidence about what precisely was done (H. S. Deighton, 'Clerical Taxation by Consent, 1279–1301' in *English Hist. Review*, lxviii [1953], 166) and it is amusing to see that the king's clerks were equally dubious. For the executors of the will of William of Louth, formerly keeper of the wardrobe, stated in a petition of 1299 that 'whereas the clergy of the province of Canterbury have granted our lord the king a fifteenth of their goods in the tenth, eleventh and twelfth years (1282–84) and the clergy of the province of York have granted him a tenth of their goods in the tenth and eleventh years (1282, 1283), and William of Balham, clerk, was appointed collector of this tenth and sent money therefrom on several occasions to the wardrobe, the clerks who were then in the wardrobe under the abovesaid keeper entered in their rolls "fifteenth" for "tenth" because they did not know the difference whereby one province gave a fifteenth and the other a tenth'. The petition was adjudged to be well founded, an admirable illustration of the need to subject official records to the same critical examination as any other records (L. T. R. Memoranda Roll, no. 70 [27 Edward I], m. 37, Easter Communia).

they were absent from parliament almost as often as they were present, and it was not until 1334 that the *praemunientes* clause became a permanent part of the writ of summons to the bishops, as it is to this day. It is something of a paradox that in less than six years afterwards the lower clergy made their grants of taxation not in parliament but in their provincial convocations; yet, as we shall see, the lower clergy continued to send their representatives to parliament until the close of the fourteenth century. When we remember that the lower clergy continued to form a distinct 'house' in the Irish parliament until the early Tudors, we may not be so ready to dismiss them so easily from consideration. For if we knew why they kept coming to the English parliament we should know more with certainty about the commons in parliament.

Before discussing the presence of the commons in parliament we should make some necessary observations. The king had always the power to summon before him the representatives of any section of his people or any part of his kingdom, whether of Jews or foresters or merchants, of shires or boroughs, at any time and at any place and for any purpose from the consideration of currency regulations or measures of defence to the planning of a new market town.[43] Knights had been summoned under John in 1213, and in 1226 they appeared as fully representative as in 1295. Burgesses came by themselves before the king in 1268 to discuss proposals for a tallage.[44] Such representative assemblies met, like parliament, at the king's command; they were, like parliament, a device of government. By royal command all representatives followed the practice, well known all over Europe by the beginning of thirteenth century, of providing themselves with full authority (*plena potestas*) to bind their constituents to whatever they did on their behalf.[45] Historians sometimes seem to suggest that they came with full power to refuse obedience, and out of

43. The definitive discussion is by A. B. White, 'Some Early Instances of Concentration of Representatives in England', *American Hist. Review*, xix (1914), 735–50.

44. G. O. Sayles, 'Representation of Cities and Boroughs in 1268', *English Hist. Review*, xl (1925), 580–85.

45. The writs for the election of borough representatives in 1268 give the precise terms of the letters to be sealed by the electors, which granted full powers of general attorney.

that misconception they attribute to them a control they never possessed. The command that representatives who came to parliament should have *plena potestas* was not a conscious and deliberate 'device evolved by Edward I's law officers'[46] to legalise general taxation: such authority had become a commonplace matter many years before he was born and, indeed, had been required by his father when he summoned borough representatives to meet him in 1268.[47] Nor was there any novelty in the phrase that appears in the parliamentary writ of summons in 1295: 'what concerns all should be approved by all'.[48] This well-known maxim proclaimed no popular sovereignty but openly recorded that the right to be consulted was accepted in government circles. But though this right had long been enshrined in feudal law and received its most dramatic expression in the stipulations of the Great Charter concerning extraordinary taxation, it did not carry with it the right to refuse. For the power to tax was part of the king's prerogative: without it he could neither defend nor govern his realm. The representatives of the lower clergy, the shires, the boroughs, the merchant classes may expostulate, dispute the amount, seek exceptions, ear-mark grants for the purpose put forward: the king may agree to some of the conditions and, as is the way in politics, then find it impossible to keep them and jettison them. All this made little difference to the final result. The England of the Middle Ages could no more than the England of 1940 withstand the argument that the safety of the state was at risk, that there was a threat of invasion, that war was inevitable and justifiable.[49]

46. Sir Goronwy Edwards in *English Hist. Review*, lvii (1942), 478, and 'The *Plena Potestas* of English Parliamentary Representatives', in *Oxford Essays in Medieval History presented to H. E. Salter*, pp. 141–54.
47. See above, n. 44.
48. The background evidence concerning this phrase as well as *plena protestas* has been presented magisterially by Gaines Post, *Studies in Medieval Legal Thought*, chaps. III and IV.
49. It should not be forgotten that the arrangements for collecting the taxes were the king's. In 1301 the manner in which the fifteenth, granted at Lincoln, was to be levied was discussed and settled, first before the king and the earls, barons, and others in his army at Glasgow, then before the king's son Edward and the earls, barons, and others in his army at Newcastle in Ayr (K. R. Memoranda Roll, no. 75 [30 Edward I], m. 52, Trinity Communia. For the form of taxation, see m. 8, Michaelmas Communia).

There was no imperative reason why elected representatives should have to come to central headquarters to assent to taxation. Indeed, the question of consent to taxation was faced and answered outside parliament long before it made its way inside parliament. For many years it was usual for a grant to be negotiated in regional or local assemblies. When it was deemed unsatisfactory in 1282, there was resort to the twin financial assemblies at York and Northampton in 1283. In 1301 the boroughs in Yorkshire were approached and asked to increase the amount of taxation they had previously approved.[50] Assemblies of merchants were frequently convened to discuss customs duties but these must be kept in the context of war finance rather than parliament. As late as 1337 an effort was made to obtain a grant by negotiating with each shire court separately.[51] Other local fund-raising missions were attempted later. To levy taxes at the local instead of the national level was the common practice in Ireland,[52] in Wales, and in France, because in disrupted countries it was the only effective way. But in England the king's writ ran throughout nearly all the land and it was obeyed, and nowhere did his authority stand uniquely higher than when he was in his council in his parliaments. If he thought it convenient and worth while he could and did summon popular representatives to appear at parliament to express their assent to a grant and facilitate its collection.[53] They came only as and because it pleased him, and he did not send for them to allow them to question his authority.[54] Out of nearly fifty parliaments held by Edward I

50. *Cal. Close Rolls*, 1296–1302, p. 462, and see below, p. 102, for procedure in 1319.

51. J. F. Willard, 'Edward III's Negotiations for a Grant in 1337', *English Hist. Review*, xxi (1906), 727–31. Presumably a grant was needed more quickly than a formal summons of a parliament would have permitted. The grant was made and paid but it was ratified in a later parliament.

52. Richardson and Sayles, *The Irish Parliament in the Middle Ages*, p. 67: in 1300 parliament advised bargaining separately with counties and franchises.

53. G. O. Sayles, 'Parliamentary Representation in 1294, 1295, and 1307' in *Bull. Inst. Hist. Research*, iii. (1925–26), 110–15: the summons of two knights to parliament who were intended to act simply in the capacity of tax-collectors.

54. There is no need to dwell upon the fanciful and unwarranted theories that have been advanced to explain the presence of the commons

knights of the shire attended fourteen, burgesses eleven. The knights represented the lesser barons whom the Great Charter had arranged to be summoned to discuss taxation, not by special but by general writ. The burgesses broadly represented the king's demesne, which had once been subject to tallage.[55] In the thirteenth century the old types of taxation like the feudal aids and tallage were rapidly vanishing. But though rigid distinctions were becoming blurred and the king taxed his subjects generally, the old conception that taxation was a matter of negotiation between the king and the various social groups in his realm lived on. When all classes were taxed, they were taxed as communities at different rates. The idea of national taxation, assessed uniformly and indifferently upon all classes, was quite foreign to medieval thinking. The normal tax became a tax on personal property, on what were called 'movables', and it was levied as a specific proportion of their value—a sixth or a ninth, a tenth or a fifteenth. By 1294 a different rate was established for town and country and by 1334 the former paid a tenth and the latter a fifteenth. And in this year, in the hope of stopping the corruption in collection which prevented the tax from bringing in as much as was expected, it was declared that it must always produce £38,000. That became thereafter the fixed ceiling and there ceased to be any further proper relationship between the wealth of the country and the amount of taxation it could bear.[56] Taxation in parliament quickly became an established tradition. The knights and the burgesses spoke by themselves and for themselves and no one else. On three occasions, in 1283, Lent 1305, and January 1307, when elected representatives attended parliaments, no question of taxation was apparently raised. It has

in parliament: they were not there to explain to the king the problems of local government and to carry home his directives, as Riess argued; they were not there to bring petitions on behalf of the community, a suggestion utterly quashed by Professor G. L. Haskins; they were not there to act as a balance to the power of the magnates, a conception that only nineteenth-century liberalism could have foisted upon so many historians, including one as iconoclastic as Professor A. F. Pollard.

55. For refinements of this generalised statement, see R. S. Hoyt, 'Royal Demesne, Parliamentary Taxation, and the Realm, 1294-1322', *Speculum*, xxiii (1948), 58-69.

56. If higher taxation was required, it was possible to ask for two tenths and two fifteenths, but this was unusual.

been suggested that they were there for publicity reasons, to celebrate the king's triumphs against the Welsh, the Scots, and the pope. There was, it is true, an imperative need for communication, a need to influence opinion, especially concerning war and its likely consequences. It seems reasonable to assume that political support was worth having on occasion, and it will assuredly become more valuable in the troubled times of Edward II.

We end this chapter on a cautionary note. So far as any thirteenth-century document is concerned, there is no suggestion, not the faintest hint, that the representatives of the lower clergy, the shires, or the boroughs were necessary to the composition of parliament or, when they were there, added anything to its authority. The doctrine that the presence or absence of representatives of the people (if that is the correct phrase when knights of the shire were often sheriffs or simply nominated by sheriffs and when burgesses came, often only at the discretion or caprice of sheriffs, from a narrowly restricted constituent body) is the criterion for deciding whether a particular assembly was or was not a parliament is utter anachronism and in the face of the evidence it is an absurdity. There was no necessary connexion between parliament and popular representation: across the Channel we see the same statement is true of France. We are compelled for clarity's sake to illustrate. The assembly of 1273 which gathered to proclaim the accession of a new king is styled by a recent historian a 'parliament', presumably because elected representatives were summoned,[57] yet a host of contemporary witnesses is in no doubt at all that the Easter parliament of 1275 was the first parliament of Edward I's reign. Then why the use of such loose language? Again, we are told that 'petitions could be and were presented at "parliaments" to which no representatives had been summoned'.[58] The double apostrophes need no comment, they speak for themselves: parliament is not a proper parliament if the commons are absent. Even a historian admirably punc-

57. By F. M. Powicke in *The Thirteenth Century*, pp. 225, and *King Henry III and the Lord Edward*, ii. 593*n* (the Winchester annalist does not, as stated, call this assembly a 'parliament' but a 'convocation'), 594.
58. H. M. Cam, *Liberties and Communities in Medieval England*, p. 224.

tilious in definitions can yet describe as 'parliament' an assembly in 1268, presumably because twenty-seven boroughs sent representatives to it: there is no contemporary justification.[59] Nor should the financial assembly at Northampton in 1283 be termed a parliament.[60] The *ne plus ultra* is reached when the parliament of 1310 in which the king authorised the barons to reform the administration of his realm is described thus: a 'pseudo-parliament, such as that of 1310 at which there were no commons representatives'.[61] In the emotional context of national myths, whether in Europe or the United States, fact is not likely to overcome fiction until it no longer matters. *Magna est veritas et praevalebit:* not the present, always the future tense.

59. Gaines Post, *Studies in Medieval Legal Thought*, p. 110.
60. J. S. Roskell in *Bull. Inst. Hist. Research,* xxix (1956), 160.
61. J. H. Trueman, 'The Statute of York and the Ordinances of 1311', *Medievalia et Humanista*, x (1956), 76.

6. The Ordinances of 1311: The Reaction against Bureaucracy

The gist of the preceding chapter may be summarised in words used many years ago which there is no reason to alter: under Edward I 'the contribution of judges, ministers and clerks to the development of parliament was out of all proportion greater than the contribution of any other body of men there represented either regularly or intermittently—barons, knights or burgesses'.[1] This is medieval bureaucracy *in excelsis*.

Under Edward II there was a remarkable change in the climate of English politics, leading to a dramatic alteration in the structure of government, and this change called for the participation of elected representatives in the functioning of parliament. Their role was assigned to them, not won by them: this statement lies at the heart of current disputations, and we shall return to it later. Edward II has been judged harshly, mainly because he has been used as a foil to his more distinguished father, and we must sympathise with him in his harassments and perplexities. For we must consider not his reign alone but the years 1297–1330, a period which is all of one piece, beginning when the rupture between Edward I and the barons became wide open and, as it turned out, irremedi-

1. Richardson and Sayles, 'The Exchequer Parliament Rolls and Other Documents', *Bull. Inst. Hist. Research*, vi (1928–29), 145. Cf. *The Mirror of Justices*, pp. 155f.: 'And whereas ordinances ought to be made by the common assent of the king and his earls, they are now made by the king and his clerks'.

able, and ending in 1330 when Edward III first began to rule
as well as reign. For Edward I had in his later years proved
himself to be as arbitrary and untrustworthy as he had been
known to be when he was a young man, and this time he was
no longer attended by success but manifest disaster: an increasing lawlessness in society at large, a country drained of its re-
sources, a church with its head, the archbishop of Canterbury,
in exile, an unnecessary war. He had, in particular, aroused
deep suspicions when he obtained permission from the pope
in 1306 to repudiate his confirmation of the charters (the
Great Charter and the Charter of the Forest) in 1297. He did
not live long enough to show the full use he meant to make
of his deliberate escape from long-established obligations, but
to the barons the future must have seemed ominous. Now,
Edward II inherited willy-nilly the evils that resulted from his
father's bad faith and it was imperative that a *modus vivendi*
should be found at once to avoid a dangerous confrontation
and achieve conciliation. Such was provided by adding a fourth
promise to the traditional guarantees [2] of the ancient coronation oath: 'Sire, do you acknowledge that you must hold and
keep the laws and rightful customs which the community of
your realm shall have chosen.' [3] Some have argued that this ad-
dition signified nothing that was new, being but a confirmation
of what had been the rule in the past; others that it was a concession obtained by the barons through coercement of the new
king and referred explicitly to the future, not the past; others
that it represented a policy of appeasement by the king, who
thus swore that what his father had done by unilaterally repu-
diating the charters would not be done again.[4] It is beyond
dispute that past traditions were confirmed: the king must
remain the supreme lawgiver but he must obtain the assent
of his natural-born advisers. The future perfect of the verb
'shall have chosen' (*aura eslu*) is not a tense that fits happily

2. To protect the Church and maintain peace; to uphold good laws
and abolish bad laws; to dispense justice to all.
3. For the text of the new coronation oath, see R. S. Hoyt, 'The
Coronation Oath of 1308', *Traditio*, xi (1955), 237.
4. For these three interpretations, see Hoyt, *op cit.*; B. Wilkinson,
'The Coronation Oath of Edward II and the Statute of York', *Speculum*,
xix (1944), 445–69; H. G. Richardson, 'The English Coronation Oath',
Trans. Royal Hist. Soc., 4th series. xxiii (1941), 129–58.

into an English sentence, but the debate whether this promise
was either proleptic or related merely to laws already agreed
or, indeed, both is somewhat futile because surely there could
be no future laws to which the king did not, however formally, assent: laws were not passed over the heads of medieval
kings and no baron, however irresponsible, would have thought
in such terms. But the following point may well have been
implied: though legislation must be the outcome of discussion between the king and the magnates, representing the
community of the realm, would it originate from above with
the king's servants, the judges and civil servants, as under Edward I, or would it originate from below with the king's subjects, as it had in 1215, in 1258, and will do again from 1327
onwards? Whether or not the new clause meant coercion or
appeasement, the political situation rapidly deteriorated: the
ineptitude of the king—shown in the foolish exaltation of his
friend Peter Gaveston—and the relentless animosity of the
barons—shown in that collapse of the rule of law that ultimately permitted Gaveston to be murdered—combined to produce the crisis of 1310 and the reform of the administration.
Early in March at Westminster the prelates, earls, and barons
presented a respectful petition to the king, setting out a series
of grievances and praying him that 'for the salvation of your-
self and of them and of the Crown (which they are bound by
their allegiance to maintain) you will agree with them that
these perils and others may be avoided by ordinance of the
baronage'.[5] The king assented to this prayer and limited the
powers of the Lords Ordainers, a group of twenty-one bishops
and nobles, appointed to reform the realm, to a period up to
Michaelmas 1311. The prelates and barons acknowledged this
limitation and declared that the king's concession was not to
be drawn into a precedent and not interpreted except as a
purely voluntary act on his part. For, indeed, his assent was
essential if the projected ordinances, when devised, were to
have any effect.

The Lords Ordainers did not look upon themselves as inno-
vators. They meant to conserve the traditions of the past as
they understood them to be and to remove ultimate control

5. For references, see J. C. Davies, *Baronial Opposition to Edward II*,
pp. 358f.

from the professional experts around the king. For they insisted that he was getting the wrong counsel from the wrong persons. There was more than a personal vendetta with Gaveston involved. The barons insisted that their advice must predominate in the king's council, especially in time of parliament. Therefore parliament was to meet once a year, if necessary twice, and it is surely evident that they had no more difficulty in knowing what was and what was not a parliament than their forefathers at Oxford in 1258. Seven parliaments had been convened in the two and a half years before the Lords Ordainers were appointed and, though arrangements had been made for a parliament at Easter 1311, none was convoked before they had submitted their final proposals to the king in the following August. Why they should have let eighteen months go by without convening a parliament can only be explained by the topsy-turvy state of affairs, for no one on either side quite knew what was going on. For example, in a letter written by the chancellor at York on 25 November 1310, mentioning that all the courts as well as the chancery were to be transferred from London to York at Easter 1311,[6] he wryly remarked:

> The prelates and the earls Ordainers who are at London are bitterly irritated and much vexed at this, and they have each gone to their several estates and have secretly arranged to meet again. But no one yet knows where or when, for which reason many people fear the worst. And so the earl of Lincoln is greatly annoyed at this assembling of the courts together and has informed our lord the king that this is neither to his advantage nor to his honour, especially at a time like the present, and that he will not have the authority to act on his behalf or to keep his peace for him after the courts are brought together in this way. But, indeed, sir, I really believe that, since the earl of Lincoln has informed my lord of the dangers that may befall thereby, the matter will be put off.[7]

Having arranged for regular sessions of parliament, the Ordainers laid down what they considered to be the business to be considered in parliament: to deal with lawsuits that had been held up because the defendants had pleaded that they

6. *Cal. Chancery Warrants, 1244–1326*, p. 329: 28 October 1310.
7. B. M. Add. MS. 25459, fol. 43. The orders were, in fact, cancelled.

could not answer without the king; to hear the grievances of
those who had suffered from the unlawful acts of the king's
ministers and officials; to consider pleas upon which the judges
were divided in their opinions; to receive and answer petitions.
These four functions precisely describe what parliament had
been doing for nearly forty years and correspond with what
the author of *Fleta* had defined a few years earlier as its concern. Parliament was to remain the highest court in the land,
the supreme tribunal for settling questions of law and administration, and it was to remain open to the lowliest of the
king's subjects. So at Hilary 1316 the chancellor, the treasurer,
the judges of the king's bench and the common pleas, were to
compile a record of all the actions pending before them 'which
cannot be determined outside of parliament' and transfer them
for adjudication to the parliament then meeting at Lincoln.[8]
And this parliament was itself adjourned and continued after
Easter 'for the answering of petitions which could not be answered on account of the shortness of time'.[9] Consequently,
the services of experienced and trained men remained essential
and the procedures for conducting and recording the business
of parliament were not altered: chancery clerks like Robert of
Ashby and William Airmyn act as clerks of parliament; receivers of petitions are drawn indifferently from chancery, exchequer, or wardrobe and chosen afresh for every parliament,
and accept petitions from England and from Gascony (to
either of which Ireland, Scotland, Wales, and the Channel
Isles were attached as convenience dictated); the panels of
auditors still sent problems to the council.

   Nothing was said about the composition of parliament.
Elected representatives had not been summoned in 1310 to
attend the parliament which initiated the reform measures and
their absence did not detract in any way from the validity of its
decisions.

   From a political point of view it is plain that the Ordainers
were determined to underline unmistakably the ancient rule
that the king must take counsel with the barons on important
issues: war and peace, the appointment of the king's chief

8. *Rot. Parl.*, i. 350.
9. Duchy of Lancaster, Royal Charters, 10/217.

ministers, grants of money, were all matters to be discussed and settled only in parliament. We can observe a greater admixture of politics, especially foreign affairs and diplomacy. There is nothing novel in this, it is simply stressing and enlarging an old function. What is novel is that the barons have let it be clearly seen that the reins were to be in their hands and not in those of the professional experts. However necessary they are for work too technical, too time-consuming, too boring for the barons as a whole, they will never again be as authoritative and as prominent as they had previously been. Their position has become anomalous, they are obviously much less important, they drop to a subordinate position. The barons between the promulgation of the Ordinances in 1311 and their annulment in 1322 asserted their own dominance in the state and that dominance was reflected in parliament. A momentous change had taken place in the governance of the country and it will work its way out by the end of the reign. A small indication of the way in which the wind was blowing was seen in the appointment of more magnates to the panels of auditors as though their presence was deliberately intended to restrict the freedom of action of the professional members. Much more significant was the emergence of what was termed 'the great council in parliament'. The council is 'great' not only because the magnates are its most prominent and dominant members or because it reviews matters of importance: it is 'great' to differentiate it from the small council composed mainly of officials. A document of 1314 makes the distinction quite clear: some members of the king's council at Westminster had been discussing events in the last parliament at Paris, whereupon 'it seemed to some of the council that such weighty matters ought to be dealt with in parliament and before the great council and by greater and more distinguished men because the business appears to pertain to them . . . for such matters are serious and should be dealt with in the presence of the earls . . . and so, for fear of offending them, the business was postponed.' [10] Again, fifteen of the twenty-three membranes of the parliament roll for 1315 are mainly taken up with proceedings before 'the great council': foreign affairs, appoint-

10. Exchequer, Parliament and Council Proceedings, file 2, no. 5.

ment of special commissions of judges, petitions.[11] Now, the
reign of Edward I had known nothing of any 'great council in
parliament'. Under him parliament could function, save in
exceptional circumstances, without the assistance of formally
summoned barons and certainly of representatives of the commons: the reign of Edward II sees the earls and barons sitting
at the centre of the seat of judgement. Under Edward I the
most prominent members of the king's council in parliament
were there because of their talents as judges and civil servants;
under Edward II men are there, because of their birth or the
dignity they hold in the Church, as prelates, earls, and barons.

The conception of peerage, with its essential basis in birth
and dignity, is now rapidly taking shape, though it had been
long evolving. When Bracton ventured the opinion that the
king's errors might perhaps be corrected in the king's court
by the community (*universitas*) of the realm and that in grave
cases of lese-majesty 'peers' ought to be associated with the
judges, he was thinking of men of high rank near the king but
he is not using the word 'peer' as a term of art.[12] But when
Fleta refashions Bracton's words forty years later, it is 'before
the court and the peers' (*coram curia et paribus*) that the
trial should take place,[13] or, to use the phrase of Britton,
another legist and a contemporary of the author of *Fleta*,
'earls and barons in time of parliament'.[14] About 1300, therefore, 'peers' are beginning to be equated in men's minds with
'earls and barons'; the equation is worked out rapidly in the
political strife of Edward II's reign, and the answer was associated with parliament. In 1317 Thomas of Lancaster declared that the matters on which the king desired his advice
should be discussed publicly in parliament and in the presence
of the 'peers of the land';[15] in 1318 the bishop of Coventry
was to receive the judgement of his peers for speaking ill of the

11. Exchequer Parliament Roll, no. 18 (printed *Rot. Parl.*, i.288–
333).

12. Cf. the phrase 'peers of the county', used in 1270 (Curia Regis
Roll, no. 192 [Trinity 1270], m. 15) and 1284 (*English Hist. Review*,
xl [1925], 229–34) and 1337 (*English Hist. Review*, lvii [1942], 478,
n. 1).

13. *Fleta*, ed. Richardson and Sayles, ii, 58.
14. *Britton*, lib. i, c. 23, 8.
15. Murimuth, *Continuatio Chronicarum*, p. 273.

king;[16] in 1321 the 'peers of the land' exiled the Despensers;[17] in 1330 it was 'by judgement of the peers and parliament' that Roger Mortimer was condemned.[18] Early in Edward III's reign—that is, in 1337—it was expressly stated that the Crown is compounded of the king as head and the peers of the land as members,[19] so the peers of the land or peers of the realm are becoming an esoteric circle of great men, the lords spiritual and the lords temporal. When they began to think of summons of parliament to them as individuals as hereditary, the doctrine of peerage was very nearly that of modern times.

The emergence of the peerage had as a corollary the emergence of the commons. It is beyond dispute that hitherto the magnates had regarded themselves as the mouthpiece of the community of the realm, as they had been, for example, in 1258. The government also looked upon them in this light when they submitted to the adjudication of the council in parliament their requests for the redress of grievances, whether by king or pope: the petition of 1301 which offered a larger subsidy in return for concessions concerning the limits of forest lands and other things; the petition of July 1309 in eleven articles which for the first time formed the basis of a statute; the series of petitions in 1318 from the prelates, earls, barons, and the whole community of the realm.[20] If commoners as commoners had a grievance, it was expressed on their behalf by the magnates: thus the sixth article in 1309 came from 'the knights and the men of cities, boroughs and other townships', complaining that, when they came to parliament, they could find no one to receive their petitions, but this article was part and parcel of the petition from 'the community of the realm'. So long as the prelates, earls, and barons insisted on maintaining the fiction of corporate action and virtual representation and looked upon themselves as the 'community of the realm' (*universitas regni*), the commoners took no concerted action.

16. Exchequer Parliament Roll, no. 21 (printed Cole, *Documents*, p. 17).
17. *Statutes of the Realm*, i. 181, 184.
18. *Foedera*, II. ii. 643f.; *Rot. Parl.*, ii. 53.
19. *Register of John de Grandisson*, ii. 840.
20. *Parl. Writs*, i. 104; *Rot. Parl.* i. 443f.; Cole, *Documents*, pp. 6f.

Out of fewer than a dozen petitions presented in parliament in the name of the people, six emanated from the magnates and there is no sign of organised petitioning from elected representatives as a group.[21] It is true, however, that their presence in parliament was becoming habitual, though not essential: after August 1311 knights of the shire attend every parliament but two (one in January 1320, the other at Midsummer 1325) and the burgesses every parliament but the same two (the assembly in October 1324, at which knights only were present, may not have been a parliament). And it was coming to be commonly believed that assent to taxation must not be sought by local agreements but negotiated only in parliament. For instance, when towards the end of April 1319 the cities and boroughs of Hampshire were asked at a meeting in Winchester to provide and equip ships for use in the north against a Scottish invasion, 'the whole community of the county replied that the mayors and the men of substance of the county had been summoned to the king's parliament at York in which, as they firmly believed, it was essential to arrange and grant a common tax throughout the whole of the kingdom in aid of the war, and they were ready to pay such a subsidy along with the rest of the country and nothing else.'[22] But even in questions of taxation knights and burgesses did not represent the same interests, for knights, as once representing the lesser barons, had always a far closer connexion with the nobility than with trade. In 1301, the petition from the 'community of the realm' was put forward by a knight of the shire, Henry of Keighley, who paid for his temerity in challenging the suspected intentions of the king by being thrown into gaol on his identification five years later and not released until 31 May 1307.[23] In 1306 the prelates, earls, barons, and knights deliberated together and granted a twentieth to the king, whilst the burgesses granted a thirtieth on their own.[24] In

---

21. G. L. Haskins, 'The Petitions of Representatives in the Parliaments of Edward I', *English Hist. Review*, liii (1938), 1–20; 'Three Early Petitions of the Commonalty', *Speculum*, xii (1937), 314–18.

22. Ancient Correspondence, vol. lv, no. 46.

23. L. T. R. Memoranda Roll, no. 76 (34 Edward I), m. 44d (51d), Trinity Communia.

24. *Ut supra*, m. 43 (printed Pasquet, *Origins of the House of Commons*, pp. 234–36).

1322 earls, barons, and other magnates and knights again contributed a tenth together.[25] But matters of taxation, however
granted, could have taken up only a comparatively small part
of the time spent by elected representatives during long sessions of parliament, and they were required to earn their expenses by doing more than the king demanded of them and to
promote the interests of their constituents, who paid not in-
considerable expenses. There was, indeed, nothing to stop
them from handing in petitions in the routine way to the parliamentary receivers on behalf of an individual shire or borough, and this they apparently did. Thus, in 1315 a protest
was made that the auditors of petitions had no power to authorise the issue of a writ, contrary to the normal chancery
practice, in answer to a petition before them, for this petition,
though ostensibly made at the request of the community of
Devon, did not originate there, 'as can be ascertained from the
knights sent to parliament for Devon'.[26] It would be hard to
interpret this protest except on the assumption that knights
representing a shire were known to present petitions on behalf
of that shire.

It is with these two developments in mind—the conception
of peerage and the growing activities of the commoners—that
we should approach the controversial subject of the Statute of
York, made in 1322, after the king, stung into action, rounded
on his enemies, destroyed them utterly at Boroughbridge, and
then removed those limitations upon his authority to which he
had been compelled in the past to agree. Of the legislation by
which the Ordinances were repealed we know more than we do
of most medieval statutes. For we have the instructions to the
draftsmen, a draft of the act, and the act itself with a preamble
by way of explanation; we have the writ sending the repealing
act to the sheriffs; we have the revised Ordinances themselves.
On this last point it is often little realised that, though the
Ordinances were abolished, yet what were considered the good
points were retained: nine of the original Ordinances were
selected and, with some modification and redrafting, were
made into a statute complementary to the act of repeal.[27] But

25. *Parl. Writs*, II. ii. 281 (69).
26. Exchequer, Parliament and Council Proceedings, file 2, no. 4.
27. *Cal. Close Rolls*, 1318–23, pp. 557–58 (*Rot. Parl.*, i. 456–57).

it is the act of repeal which is known as the Statute of York and to which a vast importance has been attached by modern historians. If we look for a contemporary and fully authoritative interpretation of it, we must surely look first at the writ which ordered the sheriffs to publish the statute in the county courts: 'Everything ordained by the Ordainers and contained in the Ordinances is to cease in future . . . while the statutes and ordinances duly made by us or our ancestors before the Ordinances were made are to remain in force, as is more fully contained in the statute promulgated thereon in our parliament.' [28] There is here, at all events, no suggestion that the Statute of York goes beyond this. But it is contended that in the statute itself the king enunciated a formula of constitutional law which marked a decisive stage in the evolution of parliament. We must repeat the final words of the statute, round which so many arguments have gathered:

> Henceforward at all times any manner of ordinances or provisions, made by the subjects of our lord the king or his heirs by no matter what authority or commission, touching the royal power of our lord the king or his heirs or against the estate of the Crown, shall be annulled and in no way have validity or force. But the things which are to be established for the estate of our lord the king and of his heirs and for the estate of his realm and his people shall be considered, agreed and established in parliaments by our lord the king and with the assent of the prelates, earls and barons, and the community of the realm, as has been the custom heretofore.

Two points should be made at the outset. The Statute of York aroused no controversy in the Middle Ages, for it passed out of the minds of medieval men and was not deemed worthy of a place in the collections of statutes they so frequently made for their own use. After printing was invented, the many Tudor editions of the statutes knew it not, and not until the mid-eighteenth century did it find itself in print.[29] We must therefore ask ourselves why we should think a statute important when so few medieval lawyers knew about it and whether we have failed to remember that our concern is first and fore-

28. *Statutes of the Realm*, i. 189–90.
29. I.e., in 1735 by William Hawkins. Cf. H. G. Richardson in *Speculum*, xxiv (1949), 72f.

most with the contemporary truth and that we should not
magnify into a political and constitutional crisis what men at
the time came to think of little moment. Again, we must not
forget that the Statute of York represented the king's views in
the hour of his greatest success, and he was first and foremost
considering his relations with barons and not with commoners.
The plain meaning of the statute is that the right of subjects,
like the Ordainers, to initiate legislation and ignore the king
was annulled and the right of the king confirmed to approve
the terms of legislation, which would be introduced in parliament and receive the assent of those present in parliament. This was how things were done in the parliament of
York itself and in the parliaments prior to the Ordinances. Normal practices were to be resumed, abnormal practices were to
cease for ever. The old order was to be restored, an old constitutional principle was restated and no new one created. The
statute was of very little consequence except as an expression
of the king's recovery of his powers. But it has been felt that
the authors of the statute had refinements in their minds:
they were distinguishing fundamental law from ordinary laws,
they were thinking of elected representatives, knights and burgesses (but curiously not the lower clergy), when they spoke of
the 'community of the realm,' and in that connexion were discussing assent to taxation rather than assent to legislation and
asserting the authority of a 'parliament of estates'. None of
these propositions is verifiable, none of them is credible. The
unwarrantable assumption that the 'community of the realm'
is synonymous with the 'commons' has met with so sharp a
reaction that it has been suggested that the use of the phrase
'community of the realm' sprang from nothing more than the
love of medieval clerks for redundant verbiage and signified
nothing at all.[30] This is too drastic a way of solving the problem created for themselves by modern historians. Once again
we would argue for a simple matter-of-fact meaning: the 'community of the realm' is present in parliament in the persons of
those whom the king has thought fit to summon for consulta-

30. J. R. Strayer, 'The Statute of York and the Community of the
Realm', *American Hist. Review*, xlvii (1942), 1–22. For the controversies
surrounding the Statute of York, see the thoughtful summary contained
in this paper.

tion.[31] The phrase covers knights and burgesses if they are present, but their absence from the parliament of 1325 did not remove, any more than the absence of the lower clergy, the 'community of the realm' from that assembly. The assent to taxation by knights and burgesses was traditionally essential if it concerned them, though it was still arguable that taxation which did not directly affect them but, for instance, only the producers and merchants of wool, was no concern of theirs. Their assent to legislation should be sought if it affected their interests, but that the king had made it absolutely essential that they initiate and assent to all legislation in general seems to defy common sense, simply because no government would voluntarily so cripple itself. There is, in brief, no proof that parliament was in the least changed by the Statute of York: it was to be what it had been before. And the belief, still asserted,[32] that the monarchy and the baronage had been competing for the support of the commons should have died with Stubbs if not with his seventeenth-century indoctrinators: it consorts ill with what kings and peers conceived to be their political and social coherence.

But a change took place in the way in which parliament functioned that owed nothing to the Statute of York but was the consequence of the two developments to which we have already referred—the conception of peers as judges and the conception of commoners as petitioners—which worked concurrently together to change the method of procedure. The prac-

31. Cole, *Documents*, p. 15: 'at the request of the prelates, earls and barons and of all others staying in the city for the parliament'; Ancient Petition, no. 10148: 'Have it shown to our lord the king and to his council on behalf of them and the good folk and the common people who have come to his parliament'. Much speculation has gathered round entries on the printed parliament rolls but it is quite essential to go beyond them and examine the unprinted petitions which lie behind these enrolments. For instance, the petition of the 'community of Devon' (*Rot. Parl.*, i.361) was presented on behalf of sheriffs, past and present (Ancient Petition, no. 174). The petition (Ancient Petition, no. 129) behind the 'community of the realm' (*Rot. Parl.*, i.372) does not reveal who the petitioners were. But behind the 'community of Kent' (*Rot. Parl.*, i.377b) lies Ancient Petition, no. 147, addressed unusually and intriguingly: 'Kent. To the lords of our lord the king's council complains the community of the said county'.

32. H. M. Cam in *English Hist. Review*, lii (1937), 320. Cf. M. V. Clarke in *Trans. Royal Hist. Soc.*, ix. 37: in the Irish parliament 'the Executive hoped to use the commoners to counterbalance the magnates'.

tice whereby prelates, earls, and barons presented petitions on behalf of the community for the adjudication of the council in parliament was anomalous when they came to predominate in the council: petitioners could not also be judges. But there now existed another way by which such petitions could be put forward. The elected representatives of shires and boroughs could well form the channel of communication instead. The peers as judges and the commoners as petitioners: this explained why parliament ceased to be a unicameral and became a bicameral institution with two separate and distinct chambers which will in time be known as the House of Lords and the House of Commons. We do not know at whose instigation the change took place or whether a petition of 'knights, citizens and burgesses on behalf of the shires, cities and boroughs of the realm', complaining in 1320 of the prevalence of crime,[33] or the petitions from 'the whole community' in 1325 [34] went to the council on their own and not through the agency of the magnates.[35] But we do know that in the revolutionary parliament of 1327 the duty of presenting petitions to the king and council in parliament on behalf of the community of the realm lay with the elected representatives, the knights and burgesses, the commons. On all counts it was a novel practice in 1327, one that had grown up during the lifetime of the men who were then in parliament. By 1399 it will seem fundamental and of remote antiquity: 'the judgements of parliament pertained solely to the king and the lords and not to the commons. . . . The commons are petitioners and demandants, and the king and the lords have for all time had and shall have by right judgements in parliament.' [36] From 1327 the new procedure made it essential that the commons should invariably be present in parliament as part of the machinery by which it worked. The outcome was not foreseen and it was not planned. But the parliament of Edward I parted company from its likeness to the parliament of Paris; it was not to be a pro-

33. *Rot. Parl.*, i.371.
34. *Ibid.*, 430.
35. Cf. the letter of a papal envoy under Edward II, possibly in 1322, addressed to 'Edward, by the grace of God the illustrious king of England and to the prelates and barons of the realm of England, holding the king's parliament' (Ancient Correspondence, vol. xxxiii, no. 93).
36. *Rot. Parl.*, iii. 427*b*.

fessional body of jurists and administrators. It was to develop as a 'parliament of estates', and return as the true successor of the old traditional 'feudal court' and become the modern parliament. The consequences were immensely important for the future. But that future, however pointed towards parliamentary democracy, was still very far distant. We have the advantage—or maybe we should say disadvantage—of hindsight and know the end of the story. But it is improbable that contemporaries saw much difference, for the changes were slow and undramatic. Of one thing they could be quite certain: the 'parliament of estates' was no different from its predecessors in being an expression of the royal prerogative and not of any 'national will'. For parliament could not do without the king, but the king could do without parliament. It still remained the king's parliament.

7. The King's Parliaments in Perspective in the Later Middle Ages

When we look backwards we see the year 1327 as marking most plainly for us a dividing line. The motive that lay behind all the changes had been political and, as parliament increasingly subserved political purposes and responded to political pressures, the balance of business brought before parliament and the methods of dealing with it were inevitably altered.

The judicial aspect of parliament never disappeared and is still with us in the jurisdiction of the House of Lords as a court of final appeal, but it began to fade out of the foreground. The old established procedures still remained, but they were used for different purposes. The clerks of the parliament continued to be drawn from the group of chancery clerks but their functions were gradually restricted to duties of a subordinate nature. They kept the roll which had begun as the roll of the council and became the sole parliamentary roll, unfortunately quite unsystematic and capricious in what it recorded. They might be required to read proclamations within parliament and to convey messages to it from the king. Their outstanding duty, however, was to receive the petitions presented by the commons, arrange for their proper expedition by the council, and read the consequent replies to the commons. Receivers of other petitions were recruited *ad hoc*, almost invariably from the 1330s from the same chancery staff, but it is noticeable that chancery clerks were excluded from the council. No appointments of receivers had been made in the Lent

and December parliaments of 1332:[1] whether the reason was
deliberate or accidental, the commons entered a protest and
never again did receivers fail to be appointed. Yet their responsibilities were rapidly reduced, and after 1332 they ceased to
write the rolls of private petitions—English, Irish, Gascon, and
the like—which had until then formed the vast bulk of our
collection of parliament rolls.[2] This did not mean that private
petitions to parliament had stopped, for it is abundantly clear
from the records of law courts and administrative departments
that they went on being presented. But it is equally evident that
the stream had been reduced to a trickle. The salient characteristic of the parliaments of Edward I—that is, the comprehensive dispensation of justice to all who sought it—had
withered. We do not know clearly why this happened. It has
been suggested that an explanation can be found in the emergence of chancery as a court of equity which, unfettered by the
strict rules of the courts of common law, could entertain private petitions that would previously have been brought to parliament. This is ingenious but not satisfactory, for the equitable
jurisdiction of chancery was hardly to be seen before Richard
II's reign, and even then it has left very little record of its
activities.[3] Indeed, in his reign the court of chancery transmitted petitions, too difficult for it to handle, to parliament to
obtain instructions, and parliament for its part expressly authorised petitions to be transferred from it to the court of
chancery. There was still too much interplay for them to be
considered as alternatives. If we may essay a conjecture why it
was no longer necessary for private petitions to come to parliament, we would point to the widespread use of petitions,
otherwise called bills, to obtain justice in central and local
courts of justice throughout England.[4] For procedure by bill
had already become so common in the king's bench that it was
forced in 1336 to split into two divisions, one being devoted
entirely to hearing bills. And bills were brought before the

1. *Rot. Parl.*, ii.65. 67.
2. The statement that the printed rolls of parliament are the record
kept by the clerk of parliament (Edwards, 'The Commons in Medieval
English Parliaments', p. 3) is a slip.
3. For a detailed discussion of the court of chancery before the
middle of the fourteenth century, see Sayles, *King's Bench*, v. pp. lxvii–
xcvii.
4. See above, pp. 76–79.

courts of the exchequer and of chancery and of the steward
and marshal as well as before special commissioners, justices of trailbaston, and justices of the peace. They are to be
found in county and hundred courts. Indeed, they were not
limited to royal courts but were used also in the courts of the
king's subjects: the council of the queen, the council of the
prince of Wales (a file of them still exists), the council of
the duke of Lancaster (at least one file survives), and of people
of lesser consequence.[5] With so extensive a system of bills in
operation, on which many treatises were already written in the
fourteenth century, there remained little need for provision to
be made, as in the past, for redress to be given in parliament,
which was summoned after 1332 less frequently than before.
Certainly receivers of petitions had no longer to be carefully
chosen in accordance with their special qualifications, and the
twelve senior chancery clerks gained a monopoly of the office:
having been rejected from membership of the council in parliament, they could in this way retain a largely honorary presence
in parliament. Similarly the auditors of petitions diminished
in authority.[6] Obviously, men experienced in administration
and law had to serve, and in 1348 or earlier the king's serjeants-
at-law were on call to give expert advice when needed. But
there is a noticeable increase in the number of prelates and
lords among the auditors: not many of them could have been
interested in listening to mere private petitions and their
appointment was intended to show the ministerial element
that the lords were in control in parliament.

As judicial work decreased, politics engrossed an ever
greater share of parliamentary time. The writs of summons had
always spoken of the need to maintain and preserve the
'state of the king' and the 'state of the realm'. While such
phrases or their like have formed the subject of learned and
subtle commentaries, it is not likely that those summoned
to parliament realised that they represented profound con-

5. Sayles, *King's Bench*, iv. pp. lxvii–lxxxvi. A massive corpus of
unprinted material on procedure by bill after 1272, both treatises and
legal actions, has been collected but is not likely now to be printed.
6. For the onetime authority of auditors, note the protest in 1315
that 'it does not seem that it was in the power of those who answered
petitions to order and authorise an unusual and prejudicial writ without
consulting the king or the great council' (Exchequer, Parliament and
Council Proceedings, file 2, no. 4).

stitutional principles. To them the categories of business
must have seemed quite straightforward: there was the business that concerned the king in person and there was the business that concerned the kingdom in general. They could not
fail to overlap at frequent points: for example, where supplies
of money were concerned; and rigid lines could not in practice
be drawn between them. What the king had to say in parliament was said on his behalf by his ministers and judges. His
ministers in parliament represent their departments; his judges
were there to render judgements and draft legislation; his
serjeants-at-law attended as his advocates in actions to which he
was a party. Serious matters of policy were discussed: relations
with France, Ireland, and Scotland, and with the pope; the
waging of war abroad and the means required to conduct it;
the most suitable methods of keeping the peace at home. All
such questions were raised by the chancellor or the chief
justice of the king's bench or the chamberlain or the archbishop
of Canterbury, but anyone else who had a particular knowledge
of the business in hand could be the official spokesman of the
king. The speeches were sometimes delivered to a full assembly of nobles and commons, sometimes to each of the groups
separately. There are many indications that separate issues were
transferred to *ad hoc* committees for discussion. For instance,
in 1340 eight such committees were set up. Most interesting
was an additional standing committee of one prelate, two earls,
and two barons to hear petitions that complained of delays of
justice in any of the king's courts. These men were to be advised by royal officials, to hold office until the next parliament,
and to adjourn to it any problems they felt they could not
settle themselves. We could hardly find a better illustration of
the association of parliament with a long tradition of justice.
The over-all picture of parliamentary activity is one of working
committees which do a great amount of work behind the
scenes and not in public session.

We turn now to discuss the part played by the commons
in parliament and, if we stay with them for an inordinately
long time, it is not because they constitute a very powerful
element in parliament but because they have been made to
protrude beyond their station and should be returned to their
proper place.

As we have already said, all medieval direct taxation was a matter of bargaining. Lay subsidies were on a par with clerical subsidies, and arguments about one can be equally well applied to the other. The attitude of the commons was like that of the lower clergy and was neither unique nor particularly remarkable: they disliked taxation, they opposed its imposition, they tried to lay down conditions, to obtain exemptions, and to evade it, they sought (but not with practical success) to appropriate supplies and audit expenditure. Like all of us today, they grumbled but they paid. They did not, of course, welcome taxation because it provided them with opportunities to exhibit their constitutional rights. Nothing would have pleased them more than that the king should live of his own and be praised by them for his prudent housekeeping. Responsibilities were never welcomed by them and, if government was good—that is, made no demands upon their pockets—they were quiescent. And by the close of the Middle Ages direct taxation, limited in its yield by out-of-date assessments, was being by-passed and kings were finding other and more lucrative sources of income than intermittent and grudging taxes from parliament: when grants of customs were made for life to Richard II and all but one of his successors, when forced loans and benevolences were forthcoming, parliament was of diminished account in taxation and we hear less and less about resistance to it. The history of taxation follows a predictable path, well marked by statistical evidence, and it is overstressed because it seems to show the commons in a gesture of nasodigitation to the government. But thereby the really significant developments are side-stepped and neglected.

This point can be illustrated if we consider the changing position of the clergy in parliament, particularly the lower clergy. We cannot assert that there was no idea of dealing in parliament with the English Church as a whole, whether for taxation, the consideration of grievances and reforms, or the discussion of general policy.[7] It is true that a single national assembly of the Church itself was a very difficult thing to

7. Across the Irish Sea the lower clergy continued to be present in parliament until the sixteenth century and voted subsidies together with the commons (Richardson and Sayles, *The Irish Parliament in the Middle Ages* [2nd ed.], pp. 118, 145, 185–86, 191).

organise in view of the ancient and bitter animosity between
the archbishops of Canterbury and the archbishops of York:
often a papal legate was needed to compel them to deliberate
together. Nevertheless such an idea was fundamentally im-
practical. For throughout the Middle Ages the Church stood
against the State as an independent and rival authority which
regarded the pope and not the king as its supreme lord. And if
the Church did not always speak with one voice, the separate
provinces of Canterbury and York had their own machinery
of government and could formulate their grievances within
their own convocations and diocesan synods and have them
presented in parliament through bishops and other prelates.
When the clergy in parliament began to insist that, before
reaching any final decision on requests for taxation, they
should first be allowed to discuss them in their own convocation, it was plainly a waste of time to duplicate procedure, and
it became the established practice for archbishops to convene
convocations in obedience to a royal writ and there authorise
clerical subsidies: occasionally, but by no means always, the
convocations of Canterbury were convoked in London to coin-
cide conveniently with the meetings of parliament at Westminster.[8] Though, when matters of taxation were transferred
from parliament to convocation, this removed the reason why
the lower clergy had been summoned to parliament at all, it is
important to note the simple fact that they did not in consequence cease to attend its meetings. Like the commons they
had other things to do there, though what exactly they did
and how remains as yet obscure. But certainly proctors of the
lower clergy were sent to parliament until the very end of the
fourteenth century,[9] and we must presume that rectories and
monastic foundations did not go on paying their not incon-
siderable expenses for nothing. Since in the absence of evidence
we must argue from the general pattern of events, their paramount interest presumably lay in the presentation of petitions.
They could, of course, make known their complaints in

8. E.g., convocation met at St. Paul's, London, on 11 March 1336,
on which day parliament was to assemble at Westminster.
9. E. C. Lowry, 'Clerical Proctors in Parliament and Knights of the
Shire, 1280–1374', *English Hist. Review*, xlviii (1933), 443–55; D. B.
Weske, *Convocation of the Clergy*, pp. 65, 78. The proctors were not
doubling duties at coincident parliaments and convocations.

convocation and hope that the prelates would see fit to bring them to the notice of parliament. But the grievances of the lower clergy were likely to be too personal, too trivial, to make much impression in convocation. In parliament they could seek redress directly, either as individuals [10] or in concert. For auditors of clerical petitions were still appointed, and petitions of the clergy as a group were still being put forward and made the basis of legislation. Since the lower clergy had a special and limited interest, they did not deliberate with the commons. But the elected representatives of the commons were in no different case from the elected representatives of the clergy in the procedure of petitioning the council in parliament. However, in the fifteenth century collective petitions of the lower clergy vanish, their proctors stayed away, their summons remained a mere formality, and the only effective voice in parliament was the voice of the archbishops and their suffragans. The history of the lower clergy in parliament shows that there was much experimenting and that it was not necessarily very intelligent: the adjustment of parliamentary practice to the needs of the country was a never-ending and difficult process of trial and error.

In the making of statutes the year 1327 serves to mark clearly a new approach. Under Edward I legislation had been imposed from above: prepared and propounded by the king's ministers and judges, it was submitted to the council, sometimes in and sometimes out of parliament. Under Edward III legislation originated from below, being founded upon the petitions of the commons. This was not an entirely new concept, for the Great Charter of 1215 had been based upon the Articles of the Barons, the Provisions of Westminster of 1259 on the requests of the baronial reformers, and, more recently, a statute of 1309 incorporated the 'petitions of the community' as expressed by the magnates. But now politics left little room for the experts whose wisdom and experience had previously been reflected in the quality of legislation. The petitions of the commons were a haphazard collection of unrelated requests and, after those had been abstracted which

10. Ancient Petition, file 57, no. 2804: a petition of Geoffrey Langton, proctor for the clergy of York diocese in parliament in 1368, requesting judicial immunity while parliament was in session.

were unacceptable to the king or called for no change in the
law, the rest were incorporated into the typical statute, following closely chapter by chapter the order and language of the
articles in the petitions.[11] Such legislation was often ill conceived, repetitive, trivial. It settled the problems of the day
but it did not inaugurate such fundamental changes as were
made under Edward I: the statutes between Edward II and
Henry VIII exhibit few great monuments of legislation. The
contrast is strikingly shown by the fact that, when readings
upon statutes became common in the Inns of Court in the
fifteenth century, the lecturers selected the subject of their
discourses from among the 'old statutes' and utterly ignored
the 'new statutes', founded upon the petitions of the commons in and after 1327. Of course, the right of initiating legislation had not passed from the king, and government measures were put through in parliament: when left to itself, the
professional's hand had not lost its cunning, as we can see from
the better-ordered and better-drafted statutes regulating the
staple and controlling wages, which are more in line with
thirteenth-century legislation. But the political change had been
made clear by the great council in parliament in 1327: 'This
request concerns a change in the law which should not be made
except with the assent of the king and of the prelates, earls and
barons and other people of the land, and if anything ought to
be done, it must be done in parliament.' [12] And the Statute of
Treason in 1352 demanded that, before the judges could con-
strue an act not mentioned in the Statute itself as treason,
they must first obtain the agreement of parliament. But we
must not exaggerate the control of parliament over legislation,
for the royal prerogative was always in command. Not only
could the king refuse his assent or drop a bill of his own de-
vising if it was opposed (which was rare), but his power to
dispense with any legislative provision was practically un-

11. It should perhaps be pointed out that the statute roll was quite
distinct from the parliament roll. For an account of the way in which
the statute roll began to be compiled, see Richardson and Sayles, *The
Early Statutes.*

12. Ancient Petition, no. 2148: printed *King's Bench*, ii. pp. clxv f.
Cf. Cole, *Documents*, p. 26: 'to change the laws of the realm requires the
greatest deliberation, and this in full parliament'. This was the answer to
a petition, presented in 1318.

limited. A medieval statute, like the statute of Provisors of
1351, was not binding in the sense that a modern statute is.
For instance, though it had been enacted in the parliament at
Northampton in 1328 that no royal charters of pardon for
homicide were to be granted except in parliament and though
the court of king's bench hesitated about allowing a royal pardon, the king and council simply declared that it was not the
king's wish that such pardons should be disallowed.[13] Legislation is in principle the king's act and he may undo what he
has done. And though as we have seen, a convention developed
that a statute should be based upon a petition of the commons,
it was manifestly impossible for government to govern if the
initiative in important bills must be left to the commons. In
the result such bills were often introduced into parliament by
government servants, though, on the surface of things, it might
be at the commons' request. As today, the executive propounded, though its proposals might be modified in the light
of criticism within parliament. It was only in minor matters of
public interest and in private bill legislation that the initiative
did not lie with the king's council or the king himself.

Whereas the commons had been originally summoned to
be consulted about taxation and give formal assent to measures
propounded to them, the most prominent of their functions
came to be connected not with supplies—only five out of a
score of parliaments between 1327 and 1336 granted taxation—
but with petitions, with bringing to the fountain of justice the
complaints of the people. This was the note struck time and
time again in the fourteenth and fifteenth centuries. In 1327
the commons had at once taken their new duties seriously.
The rates of payment for their attendance ceased to vacillate
and were fixed at four shillings a day for a knight of the shire
and two shillings a day for a burgess, with travel expenses according to the distance of their constituency from the place
where parliament was meeting.[14] The commons knew that
men who had no right to do so had for some years past been

13. King's Bench Roll, no. 285, m. 4, crown: printed *King's Bench*,
iii. p. cxviii.
14. In May 1322 the daily rates had been respectively three shillings
and twenty pence and in March 1324 three shillings four pence and
twenty pence.

taking it upon themselves to petition as it were in the name of
the community of England, hoping that greater importance
would be given to their private complaints if they asserted
that they were voicing a national grievance. Protests against
this misrepresentation had been made in 1315,[15] and the commons decided that 1327 was the time to end it by identifying
the petitions which they as a body were prepared to support.
Therefore they put forward their requests in the form of an
'indented' bill and disavowed any other petition presented in
the name of the community. But though the commons presented such common petitions—and under Edward III a substantial part of the single parliament roll was taken up with
them—we must not imagine that they had a monopoly therein:
many 'common petitions' came from other sources, for example the clergy. But before the middle of the fourteenth century
all followed the same route in being received by the clerk of
the parliament and handed by him direct to the council for
its decision. In sharp distinction were the private petitions of
individuals or individual groups which went to the council by
the slower route of receivers and auditors and were not enrolled but filed. Yet once the commons had established themselves as one means of direct and speedy approach to the
council, then private petitioners sought to make use of them as
a preferable alternative: they might be able to persuade the
commons that their requests and grievances affected more
than themselves and should be treated as promoting a public
interest. It does not seem to have been difficult to get the
commons to sponsor such petitions as could make out a *prima
facie* case. The commons thus became co-ordinate with the
auditors as a tribunal to hear private petitions and it had the
additional advantage of immediate access to the council. Sometimes a petitioner tried both routes.[16] In the circumstances
there was room for astute lawyers to set up a 'parliamentary
practice': by getting themselves returned as members of parliament they could plead their clients' causes before the commons and get them adopted. This happened so frequently
that it was felt an abuse had been created and the lawyers were

15. See above, p. 103.
16. E.g., Ancient Petitions, nos. 4569 and 4578, presented in 1394.

accused of 'arranging to present various petitions to parliament
in the name of the commons which do not concern them'.[17]
As a result lawyers who practised in the king's courts were
disqualified in 1372 from acting as knights of the shire. But
the embargo was ineffective: nothing keeps lawyers out of parliament. So people of importance—but not poor people—such
as earls and barons, bishops and abbots, merchants and ship-
masters, and communities of single shires and towns, sent
their petitions to the commons in the certainty or hope that
they would adopt them. If they were successful, their petitions
became 'petitions of the commons', but they were not 'common petitions' in the sense that they promoted the public
welfare: acceptance by the commons did not convert a private
petition or bill into a public petition or bill, for though they
had approved and forwarded, they had not formulated. Still,
they were prepared as a body to take responsibility of some
kind for the petitions of private persons, and by the time of
Richard II petitions could be addressed not to the king or the
king in council but without disguise to the 'commons of England'. By the fifteenth century the number of petitions drawn
up by the commons on their own behalf formed a relatively
small proportion of all those they rather haphazardly accepted
and presented, and it was eventually thought that all parliamentary petitions, whether common or private, must be referred to the commons for consideration and that every parliamentary decision, even on a private petition, ought to receive
the assent of both commons and lords. The Lancastrians and
Yorkists produced little legislation of note, yet quietly and
unobtrusively over the century procedures were worked out
that ultimately gave us public acts of parliament based upon
common petitions and private acts of parliament based upon
individual petitions, the first, second, and third readings before
the commons and the lords,[18] and other such sophistications.
To the country at large the chief service rendered by the commons lay in the facilities they provided for petitioning the
Crown and obtaining an answer. It was through such work that

17. *Rot. Parl.*, ii.310.
18. A bill might require and be given more than three hearings:
the limitation to three did not become final until the close of the sixteenth
century.

they learned how to argue and debate and reach considered conclusions and by comparison with it their discussion of taxation was brief, intermittent, and destined by the end of the Middle Ages to be largely by-passed. An economic and social effervescence was apparent everywhere and the government was not unaware of it. The commons gained an increasing importance in the fifteenth century, far surpassing their position in the previous century, and, though the advance was slow, it was not incompatible with the objectives of Henry VIII when he adopted the procedure which was destined to exalt the commons in parliament.

Unity of action by the commons had been the result of pressure from above and not from within. It was the king who by the traditional obedience of his subjects to his authority over many centuries had been able to compel the commons to act together, first as taxpayers and then as petitioners. For they were not a fully homogeneous social group, even in the fifteenth century. The knights had long been a class apart as county gentry whose ties were with the nobility.[19] The distance between a noble lord and a noble knight was far narrower than between a knight and the common run of mankind. Indeed, a man could be elected to serve in one parliament as a knight and be required at another parliament to serve among the peers.[20] For purposes of taxation they did not represent the same interests as those of the burgesses and they acted independently in such matters and paid a different rate. They took precedence, were paid twice as much in wages, and were separately consulted: in 1343 the knights 'and the commons' discussed proposals for peace with France; in 1348 the knights 'and others of the commons' deliberated upon the conduct of war; in 1353 one copy of a document was given to the knights and another to the burgesses.[21] The political and social separateness is vividly revealed by the petitions addressed in

19. J. S. Roskell, 'The Social Composition of the Commons in a Fifteenth-Century Parliament', *Bull. Inst. Hist. Research*, xxiv (1951), 169: 'the ties between many of the parliamentary knights and members of the peerage were only the natural outcome of the fact that the landed gentry class was hardly distinguishable from the lower ranks of the titular nobility'.

20. Sir Thomas Camays in 1383 (*Complete Peerage*, ii.507f.).

21. *Rot. Parl.*, ii. 253, 257.

Richard II's reign to 'our lord the king, his most wise council, and the knights of the counties for the commons of England'[22] or 'to the most gracious lords and knights of all the counties of England in this parliament assembled'.[23] The most intimate picture—and regrettably the only one we have—of the discussions of the commons in the Chapter House in Westminster Abbey in 1376 shows the knights alone making all the speeches and acting as hosts at the banquet concluding the parliamentary proceedings.[24] The management of business in the 'common house' was plainly casual and haphazard. It is true that by 1363 the commons had a clerk, Robert Melton, to assist them: he was a chancery clerk, appointed by the government. And though they had a spokesman, William Trussel, in 1343 to state their views to the king and to the lords, he was neither a knight nor a burgess but in the king's service. Indeed, as it has been aptly said, the speakers continued to be speakers for the king to the commons rather than speakers for the commons to the king until at last they chose one of themselves, naturally always a knight.[25] The real unity of the commons was seen when the burgesses became genteel and members of the landowning classes. Doubtless there had always been men of substance among the burgesses, and knights were sometimes town representatives as early as Edward II's reign.[26] But the real assimilation took place over the fifteenth century. The knights were always, or nearly always, gentlemen, and gentlemen began to look upon membership of the commons as desirable and honourable. The invasion of borough seats by the county gentry was well on its way by 1422, and by the middle of the fifteenth century half of the burgess members were not truly burgesses.[27] The process did not work in reverse, for prosperous merchants and prosperous lawyers

22. Ancient Petition, no. 6869 (printed Sayles, *King's Bench*, v. p. cliv).

23. Ancient Petition, no. 5012.

24. V. H. Galbraith, *The Anonimalle Chronicle*, p. 94.

25. J. S. Roskell, 'Sir Peter de la Mare', *Nottingham Medieval Studies*, ii (1958), 36, incorporated later (1965) in *The Commons and Their Speakers*, p. 72.

26. Matthew Crowthorne in Devon and William Slyne in Lancashire (H. G. Richardson in *Bull. John Rylands Library*, xxii (1938), p. 18, n. 2; *Parl. Writs*, Alphabetical Index, p. 1435).

27. Roskell, *The Commons in the Parliament of 1422*, p. 133.

went up in the social scale to become belted knights, and it is very seldom that we find merchants as merchants sitting in parliament to represent a shire. No burgess was ever chosen as speaker in the Middle Ages, and it is quite evident that the burgesses as a group were never disposed to take a line of their own. So the personnel of the commons belonged more and more to the same class in society and the distinction from burgesses became blurred. Maybe this change resulted from a quickening interest in politics, but the reasons are much more complex, being rooted in the transformed character of fifteenth-century society which saw an increasing urbanity, the recognition of the four Inns of Court as places of general education fit for a gentleman, the attractions of London. Certain it is that we must never separate parliament as an institution from the society which placed its stamp upon it.

The county gentry and to a much lesser degree the burgesses admittedly stood high in local society, possessed much experience in local government, and attended parliament frequently. It is therefore taken for granted that they must have exercised a great—some even suggest a dominant—influence in parliament. This suppressed premise has always been at hand to colour the evidence and supply it whenever it was missing. But such a premise must, like all others, be submitted to 'the pragmatic test of recorded evidence': [28] when so examined, it remains still an unverified assumption. The parliament rolls record only the proceedings before the lords, and from them we have to extract information about the occasions when the government required the commons to select a few of their number to prosecute their petitions before the lords or to 'intercommune' with them in discussions on government proposals. The commons had been summoned for consultation: what would be surprising would be evidence that nevertheless they did not participate in 'intercommuning'. And it is wrong to believe that even the 'common petitions' necessarily represented the views of the commons themselves: it is the historian's business to look for the cause behind the cause and by closer study to discern at whose prompting the commons put

28. Sir Goronwy Edwards, 'The Commons in Medieval English Parliaments', p. 12, citing H. G. Richardson, 'The Commons and Medieval Politics', *Trans. Royal Hist. Soc.*, 4th series, xxviii (1946), 28.

forward their requests.[29] We know very little about what took place before the commons. To Chaucer and others they were ineffectual chatterers[30] and no dispassionate contemporary observer noticed any enduring qualities of leadership in them. Indeed, it seems to be assumed that repeated attendance was all that was required to turn a fool into a man of wisdom. If so, the Middle Ages had an alchemy we no longer possess. Such perception was left to nineteenth-century historians. About the affinities of the commons with the lords we have a mass of precise evidence and it stands in the most striking contrast with the poverty of precise evidence about any independence of their own. The lords and commons were largely members of one social class and a common ethos surrounded them. They could be critical of one another, disapprove of this lord or that, but their quarrels took place within a closed circle. The knights as county gentry were the more disposed to follow the lead of the lords, whose influence has been traced in shire elections.[31] Much has been written about territorial ties between them, which were very difficult to break, and about personal ties which, it is suggested, were easily broken, though Peter de la Mare, the speaker in the parliament of 1376, however public-spirited and able and popular he may have been, was not likely to oppose the earl of March whose steward he was. Under Edward III, and particularly in the fifteenth century, many of the knights of the shire came from the ranks of the royal household or were in some way or other employed in the royal service. But a binding force that was much more powerful was social sentiment, and social senti-

29. Cf. G. L. Harriss in *English Hist. Review*, lxxviii (1963), 653: 'that the traditional demand for a magnate council [in 1340] had been made through a commons petition . . . affords striking evidence of the commons' importance at this date as active agents in the great affairs of the realm'. See *Rot. Parl.*, ii. 237b: in 1352 the commons referred to 'the advice of some of the magnates sent to them regarding an aid as well as on the making of petitions touching the common people of the land'.

30. *Mum and the Sothsegger* [i.e., the Dumb and the Truth-teller], ed. Mabel Day and Robert Steele, cited Cam, *Liberties and Communities*, (1944), pp. 233f.

31. K. B. McFarlane, 'Parliament and "Bastard Feudalism"', *Trans. Royal Hist. Soc.*, 4th series, xxvi (1944), 56ff. This paper provides no evidence for its assumption that men, prominent in local affairs, must have been equally prominent in national affairs.

ment made much of distinction of rank then, as it still does in England today.[32] Explain the practice how we may, the fact remains that the genteel commons followed the lords. And this apart, we must bear it in mind, when we speak so easily of the indispensability of the commons in the governance of England,[33] that they were also dependent on the will and caprice of the king. They came when he ordered it; they went away when he so desired: so it was at the end of the Middle Ages when Henry VII found he could do without parliaments, and so it will remain until the Revolutionary Settlement of 1688. The medieval parliament was not a self-perpetuating corporation.

The extent of the influence of the commons can be tested when we consider, first, the position of the peers of the realm in parliament and, secondly, the use of great councils as an alternative to parliament. But before turning to these two subjects we may perhaps spare a few words for the reign of Henry IV, since the myth of 'Lancastrian constitutionalism', though at last exploded, still lingers on to colour and distort the evidence. Henry IV was a ruler of little competence: he did not know how to reform the abuses with which Richard II had been charged or how to raise money for his extravagant household. Furthermore, he was in the constant opinion of contemporary Europe a disreputable adventurer and a *parvenu*. He was desperately eager for recognition abroad. Hence he magnified for outward show the significance of the commons in parliament and in an endeavour to impress the French he had the speaker's seal affixed to manifestoes in order to demonstrate the popular support he enjoyed. His appeals to the commons are not a measure of the precocity of English political ideas but of Henry's weakness and insecurity. His wooing of them encouraged them to resist taxation. But we shall look in vain

32. Petitions in the late fourteenth and fifteenth centuries were addressed 'To the very gracious lords and knights of all the counties of England, assembled in this present parliament, supplicate the liege commons of the realm most humbly and request'; 'To our lord the king and his most wise council and to the knights of the counties for the commons of England'; 'To the worshipful speker and to all the knights and commons of this present parliament' (Ancient Petitions, nos. 5012, 6870, 9883). Such petitions raise problems of procedure that cannot be discussed here.

33. See below, p. 132.

for any later parallel to Henry IV's subservience, which is no more than a curiosity of parliamentary history without any later significance. In later reigns the commons sank back into their historical role as petitioners voicing grievances, discussing taxation, serving as instruments in executing the will of the king and the lords.

Unless we take the curious line of argument that those who made petitions were more important than those who had the power to grant them, we cannot fail to mistake the dominance of the lords under Edward III, and this dominance continued throughout the Middle Ages. The commons did not oppose it but rightly saw in it the traditional protection against tyranny. When the nobles relinquished the role of representing the community at large and it was given to the commons, this assuredly did not mean that they surrendered the control over parliament they had so recently gained. The commons never obtained the initiative and they obediently fulfilled the functions they were assigned in the working of the parliamentary machine. They represented a mode of procedure, but they had no independent control over it. The lords took command of it whenever they thought fit. Parliament, then as now, reflected the party in power: therefore the petitions formulated by the commons did the same. When they impeached Michael de la Pole, the chancellor, in 1386, they were not acting on their own nor did they examine with any care the charges they were induced to prefer against him. They were the tools of the fallen chancellor's enemies. In 1388 they willingly impeached in the Merciless Parliament anyone singled out by the Lords Appellant, and the decision to commit judicial murder should hardly be applauded as 'an assertion of the ultimate sovereignty of parliament'.[34] A few years later the commons were as willing to undo the work of the Merciless Parliament as they had been willing to do it. When they thus gave support to apparently contradictory policies, it is not they who have changed their mind but those in power who are manipulating the stereotyped petitory procedure of parliament. Opinion may thus be swung in parliament and dissident lords may dominate in one and the king in another. The faithful commons followed

34. T. F. Tout, *Chapters in Medieval Administrative History*, iii.432.

wherever the stronger might lead: they were not there to construct policy, a task for which they had declared themselves unfit,[35] and independent opposition was quite out of the question. If they sought to secure their wishes, they had to get the backing of the lords. There is, indeed, no historical reality in the suggestion that the commons met the lords on terms of equality in discussing matters of minor, if not major, concern. That they were subservient, that they remained to the end as they began, outside the council in parliament, that they continually failed to fulfil the high mission which modern historians demand of them—this is quite clear from the evidence and is far from being an 'unverified assumption'.[36]

The fifteenth century fully disclosed how far parliament and parliamentary procedure could be made the instruments of aristocratic factions and how much the commons acquiesced in aristocratic control. We might, indeed, get closer to the facts if we spoke, not of Lords and Commons, but of Peers and People. No single element, apart from the king himself, was so significant as the lords. We can mark some of the stages in the evolution of peerage as the lords assumed an increasingly privileged position but we have no contemporary enactment to tell us what constituted a peer or whence his powers were derived. This we must learn from the impact of events. Silent forces narrow the qualification and eventually establish a strictly hereditary peerage. The effect was to continue a limitation upon the powers of the king, a limitation accepted as a necessary condition of government. This limitation might be exercised in parliament but, as we shall see, it could be exercised equally forcibly in great councils. For contemporaries did not think in terms of parliamentary government, and want of governance did not spring from the infrequency of parliaments; indeed, when administration grew stronger and better, parliaments became fewer.

35. *Rot. Parl.*, iii. 145–48: on the issues of war and peace the commons stated in 1382 that it did not become them to give advice and asked the king with the advice of his council to do what was best and discharge them from having to answer.

36. Sir Goronwy Edwards, *op. cit.*, 18. In 1437 the commons, before their departure from parliament, referred petitions, both common and individual, to a committee of lords, ministers, and judges for adjudication by them (*Rot. Parl.*, iv. 506b).

The salient feature of the later Middle Ages was not parliament but the counsel of the lords, wherever it was expressed.
The preservation of the balance between the power of the
king and the power of the lords is the sum total of medieval
'constitutionalism', and the dilemma, caused by the dual functions of the lords, namely that they had not only to form part
of the government but at the same time to uphold resistance to it, was always well recognized. 'The magnates are the
king's right hand (*membrum regis principale*) and without
them the king cannot attempt or accomplish anything': so
wrote a biographer of Edward II.[37] Parliament in November
1330 was convoked 'with the counsel and assent of the prelates
and nobles', as was the December parliament of 1332. This
counsel was an essential element in the fabric of government.
The bishop of Exeter wrote under Edward III that 'by its nature the substance of the Crown lies primarily in the king's
person as head and in the peers of the land as members . . .
and in this way the Crown is so conditioned that there cannot
be severance without dividing the kingship'.[38] A century later,
in 1427, it was recorded that the execution of the king's authority during a minority 'belongeth unto the lords spiritual
and temporal of his land at such time as they be assembled in
parliament or in great council' and, if they are not so assembled,
then 'unto the lords chosen and named to be of his continual
council'.[39] And again, 'the king is intrinsicate within his council and may not do without them'.[40] The basic idea is, of
course, the same from the eleventh century onwards. It is a
political conception, not a legal conception, but it is the conception of men who did not contemplate any divergence of

37. N. Denholm-Young, ed., *Vita Edwardi Secundi*, p. 28. This
authoritative biography speaks only of the aristocracy and makes no
reference to the representatives of the people. It will be remembered
that high politics were discussed at meetings of the council which were
not parliaments: e.g., the council at Eltham in 1330 where, in the presence
of the archbishop of Canterbury 'and other prelates and nobles of our
realm, whom we caused to be assembled there and then on account of
our great and pressing business, the business concerning us and the king
of France was, among other matters, expounded' (*Foedera*, II. ii. 783.
And see below, pp. 129–31.
38. *Register of John de Grandisson*, ii.840.
39. *Procs. Privy Council*, iii.233.
40. Cited Richardson in *Trans. Royal Hist. Soc.*, 4th series, xxviii
(1946), 25.

aim between the king and themselves, for their common purpose was to govern the country. The reality of the principle that
monarchy should be limited by peerage depended upon the
personality of the king and the strength of individual peers.
Unfortunately the war with France had increased too much the
political and social power of the lords, and the issue between
them came to be in the fifteenth century not a balance of
power but family politics and dynastic rivalries: who should be
king? That issue was decided by the lords, either in the council chamber [41] or on the field of battle. No participant in the
conflict, claimants or usurpers alike, was deflected from his
course by a vote in the 'common house', nor were the commons consulted until after the decisive event had taken place.
In this aristocratic turmoil, not unique to England but part of
the contemporary European pattern, parliament merely regis-
tered the decrees of the victors. But in dividing themselves
into partisans of Lancaster and York, the peerage committed
suicide and left the monarchy free to become a Tudor
absolutism.

It has been reckoned that the peerage in the mid-fifteenth
century comprised some fifty spiritual peers and fifty temporal
peers and that, since only half the bishops attended parliament and few abbots and priors, and the main presence was
that of the upper ranks of the nobility, the 'lords' house was
little more than the 'continual council' writ large and suffered
in effectiveness when compared with the steady membership
of the 'common house'.[42] However reluctant we may be to

41. The overriding need for the fifteenth century is a history of the
council that will correspond with the history of the exchequer in
the twelfth century and reveal the true dynamic of government. For the
aristocratic council, whether in parliament or great council or outside
them, constituted the government when control at the top was at sixes
and sevens and obviously going to pieces. In its endeavours to control
disorder it was clearly trying to do what the Tudor council did.
42. J. S. Roskell in *Bull. Inst. Hist. Research*, xxix (1956), 153ff.
Since the Lords House settled policy and the continual council saw to
administration in detail, there was inevitably a close connexion between
them. Cf. T. F. T. Plucknett, 'The Place of the Council in the Fifteenth
Century', *Trans. Royal Hist. Soc.*, 4th series, i (1918), 173: 'In point of
actual composition, the great council and continual council at times seem
identical, but still we cannot say that they are the same, even in such
circumstances, for the two bodies are referred to by contemporaries as
being quite distinct'. According to A. F. Pollard (*English Hist. Review*,

accept a statistical approach and estimate influence by counting heads, it becomes inapplicable when we consider the 'great councils', to which the commons were never summoned in the fifteenth century.

Just as, for understanding's sake, it is imperative for a history of clerical celibacy to be accompanied by a history of clerical concubinage, so we must not write a history of parliaments without writing also a history of great councils, for these two were regarded at the time as alternative methods of conducting the business of government. To say this is to part company with the traditional view that the king must govern by parliament and that it was 'unconstitutional' for him to do otherwise. To this procrustean bed historical facts have been made to fit, no matter how distorted they became in the process. But this is not the way in which medieval kings and statesmen thought. Their overriding concern was how best to administer the affairs of the kingdom, and they were not preoccupied with parliament. To the administrator 'parliaments' were no more sacred than 'statutes' were to the lawyers who lumped them together with the common law without realising that they ought to have looked upon them as sacrosanct. We must study parliaments and great councils apart and not confuse them if we are not to foist upon the evidence ideas that were never in the head of any contemporary.

Afforced councils, other than parliaments, have a long history in England.[43] Under Edward III afforced councils were held to which knights and burgesses were summoned, and this fact has caused confusion among constitutional historians who have been unable to distinguish such great councils from parliaments or, rather, from what they imagined parliaments to be. Indeed, it has been argued that, since elected representatives attended parliament, wherever elected representatives are, there also is parliament.[44] This logical fallacy has been accepted by

---

lvii, 53), the average attendance of lords in parliament even in Elizabeth's reign was no more than thirty-five.

43. See above, chapter 2, especially p. 32.

44. T. F. T. Plucknett, 'Parliament', in *The English Government at Work*, 1327–36, i.87: 'Of these twenty-five assemblies, four may immediately be set aside for no commons were summoned to them'. It should be observed that Professor Plucknett worked from the evidence in print and the vast field of unprinted sources was little known to him

historians.[45] Yet in contemporary records parliaments and great
councils are distinguished carefully;[46] though occasionally they
are described not as 'great councils' but as 'councils' or 'trea-
ties',[47] they are recognisable in their context. The distinction
between parliaments and great councils (or general councils) is
well known to Scottish historians[48] and it is well-known to Irish
historians.[49] Only to English historians, determined to keep
parliament by itself in the forefront, is there a distinction
without a difference. Apparently the Middle Ages in English
history has a monopoly of confused and meaningless phraseology about its institutions: in modern times the confusion continues but it is then permitted to become explicable.[50] When
a convocation of the clergy is termed a 'parliament', we do
not argue for their substantial identity on the ground of no-
menclature. Indeed, it is impossible to imagine that, when the

---

(see above, p. 19, n. 38). Cf. the remark of Sir William Twysdon in the
first half of the seventeenth century: 'Wherever we find the people said to
be joined in any action with the king and nobility in councell, I cannot but
think that [to be] an assembly of the three estates which we call a
parlyament' (*Certaine Considerations upon the Government of England*,
ed. J. M. Kemble [London: Camden Society, 1849], p. 121).

45. Faith Thompson, *A Short History of Parliament*, 1295–1642,
p. 5.

46. Richardson and Sayles, *Parliaments and Great Councils*, pp. 4–5.
Ancient Petition, no. 2262, distinguishes between a petition in the parliament of February 1328 and the consequent charter, granted at the 'treaty'
of York in July 1328. And Ancient Correspondence, vol. xxxvii, no. 206,
distinguishes between the great council at Northampton in July 1338 and
the previous parliament in February 1338.

47. A 'great council' must not be confused with 'the great council
in parliament' (see above, pp. 99–100). We may have here an explanation
of the early reluctance to use 'great council' as a term of art. When in
the late fifteenth century the 'great council in parliament' had become
the 'lords', the term 'great council' shed its ambiguity.

48. J. D. Mackie in *English Hist. Review*, xl (1925), 425–27:
'Parliament, with its forty days' summons and its formal constitution,
and the less solemn, but more practical, general council . . . are found
. . . to have almost the same powers.'

49. Richardson and Sayles, *The Irish Parliament in the Middle Ages*.

50. Robert Blake, *The Unknown Prime Minister*, p. 302n: 'The
distinction between 'committee' and 'council' in the contemporary letters
and documents is frequently disregarded. The words are often used
indiscriminately and the context has to be examined before it is clear
what exactly is meant'. Similar difficulties confront the Irish historian
over the precise meaning of the king's council in the sixteenth century
(D. B. Quinn, ed., *Calendar of the Irish Council Book*, 1581–96, pp.
97f., 101).

government was able to choose between summoning a parliament and summoning a great council, it saw no difference between them. Nothing could be plainer than the proposal of the king's council in 1324 'that the magnates should be summoned to be here in order to advise etc. and not for parliament'.[51] Great councils were never formalised in composition. Even when popular representatives were summoned to them between 1327 and 1353, it was not according to any fixed plan: on one occasion only the commons south of the river Trent were ordered to attend, on another occasion only one knight from each shire and one burgess from each borough were present. It is not surprising that similarities in the form of summons, in composition, in functions, occasioned loose descriptive terms at times, but when accuracy was essential it is manifest that contemporaries at least did not regard a great council as a parliament.[52] As we have suggested, what distinguishes parliament from all other courts and assemblies is the general freedom to approach the king.

One of the purposes of the nine great councils to which the commons were summoned under Edward III was to discuss matters of taxation. But this was far from being their sole purpose: legislation might be promulgated, important questions of administration concerning the wool trade or wartime regulations decided, petitions received,[53] and actions at law determined. For many purposes a great council is, as we have said, an alternative to parliament: witness the specific instructions in 1339 to the chancellor and treasurer 'to cause to be assembled either a parliament or else a council of the magnates and those of the community' for the purpose of raising a subsidy.[54] The difference between a parliament and a great council at this period was that in a great council petitioners were given no assurance of an answer, for there is no

51. Chaplais, *War of Saint Sardos*, pp. 134f.
52. See n. 46 above.
53. In the council of September 1327 the commons seized the chance to present a common petition (Ancient Petition, no. 13018; printed *King's Bench*, v. p. cxxxii f.), but it is not always noticed that it was not answered but forwarded for consideration at a meeting of the king's council at York, possibly at Pontefract in November. For petitions of knights and burgesses in the undoubted great council of 1353, see *Rot. Parl.*, ii. 252a.
54. Chancery, Parliament and Council Proceedings, file 7, no. 10.

evidence that receivers and auditors were appointed as they were in the case of parliament, and they had in consequence no incentive to attend upon a great council as they attended upon a parliament.

Great councils with a representative element came to an end in 1353. The main purpose in this year had been to obtain the assent of the magnates and commons to certain ordinances governing the staple and to the continuance of the subsidy on wool, hides, and woolfells. The commons requested that the legislation which had been agreed should be recited at the next parliament and entered on the parliament roll 'to the intent that ordinances and agreements made in councils shall not be of record as though they had been made by common parliament'.[55] Clearly, if this principle were accepted, great councils could not profitably be used for the purposes of taxation and legislation, and the experiment of summoning great councils with representatives from shires and boroughs[56] was abandoned.[57]

But great councils without elected representatives continued to be convened, and the lords attended them as readily—or unreadily—as they attended parliament. Knights might be required to be present but they came by personal summons only. They were a less cumbersome and more expeditious way of transacting business which would otherwise have come before a parliament. In 1386 Richard II informed Pedro IV of Aragon that complaints about the unlawful seizure of the goods of Aragonese merchants would be dealt with 'at our next parliament or great council'.[58] We are informed that under Henry IV great councils 'were probably held at least as often as parliaments' and that a great council might sit off and on

55. *Rot. Parl.*, ii. 253, 257.

56. The number of representatives was not fixed as for parliaments but fluctuated: above, p. 131.

57. The great council at Winchester in 1371 was a continuation of the preceding parliament and was intended to complete the work of that parliament.

58. Perroy, *Diplomatic Correspondence of Richard II* (1933), p. 41. It would be a great service if someone would analyse the use of the term 'great council' in the fourteenth and fifteenth centuries in the same way as A. B. White analysed the term 'common council' in the twelfth and thirteenth centuries—and thus destroyed a traditional myth (see above, p. 25, n. 12).

for nine weeks,[59] but the implications of such statements vis-à-vis parliament do not seem to be fully realised. A great council, formally summoned, was still considered a good substitute for a parliament: in 1402 a parliament was cancelled and a great council summoned instead in order to despatch the business speedily with the least trouble for 'our people'. Three great councils were intercalated between the parliament dissolved in February 1440 and that which met in Lent 1442, and these five assemblies were evidently considered to be similar items in one uniform series. Indeed, both parliaments and great councils had the same clerk and he regarded them not only as clearly distinguishable but as generally equivalent.[60] This is what we would expect when parliament was but one vehicle for the counsel of magnates.

What kept parliament alive was not any statutory obligation upon the king to summon it: the prescriptions that there should be at least three a year, as in 1258, or at least one, as in 1311, 1330, and 1362, were not binding for very long. It became the accepted convention that the grant of general taxation—tenths and fifteenths, subsidies on wool or wine or in exceptional circumstances—and the enactment of statutes, indicating a supreme judicial competence in, for instance, pardoning attainders, were matters solely for parliament. But the idea that parliament was exclusively competent to perform certain functions had been a slow growth since the time when everything that could be done in parliament could be done outside parliament, when all was the act of the king and no one could legally restrain him if he chose to flout the sanctity of custom. And what if the king did not depend mainly on parliamentary taxes but derived most of his income from other sources and had little desire for statute-making? The answer was given by Henry VII when he ruled for so many years without parliament and continued to summon great councils which discussed momentous issues and even authorised financial measures to deal with them.

59. J. L. Kirby, 'Councils and Councillors of Henry IV, 1399–1413' in *Trans. Royal Hist. Soc.*, 5th series, xiv (1964), 36, 57.
60. Richardson and Sayles, *Parliaments and Great Councils*, pp. 20ff.; Perroy, *Diplomatic Correspondence of Richard II*, pp. 41, 199–200. Matthew Hale, *Jurisdiction of the Lords House of Parliament*, contains many perceptive comments upon parliaments and great councils.

Parliament was an expedient of government, to be summoned when the king desired a particularly full and representative council. But without infringing any rights or inflicting any wrongs the king may transact business at great councils, summoned in a less formal way, acquiring no technical definition, and with less notice than parliament was wont to require.[61] It has been calculated that between 1400 and 1460 forty to fifty 'great councils' met and twenty-two parliaments.[62] Such great councils were dominated by peers, and those of lesser rank who might be summoned were not elected by counties or boroughs. In his choice between these alternatives the king was only slightly hampered by the convention which gave parliament a higher status, a formal and established position, and by the limits of what it was necessary and politic to do by general assent. Otherwise the king was under no necessity to convene parliament or consult the commons. In time the intervals between parliament and parliament could run into two or more than three years, as in 1456–58 and 1478–83. At the close of the Middle Ages Henry VII summoned only seven parliaments in the whole of his reign from 1485 to 1509: in the last twelve years he summoned only one. But he summoned great councils and employed them in conjunction with parliament, not in opposition to it. The border-line between the functions of parliament and of council was indistinct (nor can we say that it is clear today). Similar neglect or indifference to parliament was shown by his son, Henry VIII. Let us state the inescapable facts starkly: no session of parliament was held in 1488, 1493, 1494, 1496, 1498–1503, 1505–9, 1511, 1513, 1516–22, 1524–29—that is, in twenty-eight out of forty-five years—and there was little protestation about the flouting of constitutional rights. Indeed, it has been said that only seventeen out of 114 public acts under Henry VII originated with the commons. The initiative in the commons house lay with the government, with the king in council. It is not simple to reconcile these figures with the statement that 'the English parliament, at the end

61. The privy seal, not the great seal, was used in summoning great councils, and a period of forty days' warning to ensure a large attendance was not required. In this connexion we should compare the contemporary practice in Scotland.

62. Plucknett, 'The Place of the Council in the Fifteenth Century', p. 165.

of the Middle Ages, had by this time met so frequently and had such important powers and traditions that the king could scarcely ignore it or work without it'.[63] For this is precisely what the two Tudor kings have done. Must we believe, no matter the facts, that the English kings recognised some constitutional imperative to summon parliament? [64] And must we also believe that the commons had an indispensable role to play in politics? [65] Parliament did not disappear as the States General were to do in France, for a quite unpredictable turn came in the tide of events and Henry VIII, faced with other possibilities, deliberately selected parliament in 1529 as an instrument to his liking and set it upon a new career as a legislative assembly, with the commons as a pliant but necessary tool for his purposes. Common assent could thereby be obtained under conditions of the fullest publicity and binding upon the whole country. He had not the slightest reason to suspect that co-operation would eventually turn into control. With so much dependent throughout the fifteenth century on accident and caprice, with so much power in the king to continue, interrupt, or break the sequence of parliaments, we must regard parliament as it was regarded then, as a device of government with an uncertain tenure of life, liable like any other such device to be outmoded and superseded or, if circumstance and convenience determined, to be remodelled and revivified. But if parliaments are an administrative contrivance for which there is often an effective alternative in great councils, if political power rests perpetually in king and peerage, if the only gainer in the contests of the fifteenth century is the monarchy, why do we concentrate our gaze on the commons in parliament and fail to look at the history of the fourteenth century without illusion and the history of the fifteenth century without

63. A. R. Myers, 'The English Parliament and the French Estates-General in the Middle Ages', in *Album H. M. Cam*, ii. 152.

64. Joel Hurstfield in *Trans. Royal Hist. Soc.*, 5th series, xvii (1967), 99: under Henry VIII there is 'no evidence that Henry VIII, Cromwell or anyone else in authority saw in parliament anything other than a useful instrument for providing revenue, for giving teeth to a strong policy, and for adding the weight of parliament to the powers and decisions of the crown'.

65. Hurstfield, *loc. cit.*, insists that the meaning of 'consent' should be properly determined. As we put it (above, pp. 122–23), we must search for the cause behind the cause and avoid surface and superficial conclusions.

disillusion? [66] For the medieval parliament ended in strong monarchical rule, not in constitutional democracy, and to 'vindicate the commons' is not the historian's primary duty.

Some day the history of parliament may be written in its own right and not as the seed-bed of representative government which at the end of the Middle Ages did not have its future behind it. If medieval institutions in their emergence and development seem to us confusing, it is because they are not corpses laid out for dissection but living organisms, for ever adapting themselves to new needs and new ends. Like life itself, the process is untidy, disorderly, apparently inconsequential. But we must avoid the fallacy of the seamless web of history, that historical continuity implies identity of function, despite the changing needs of society. Those accustomed to think in terms of a written constitution and of fundamental law may not readily appreciate the way in which parliament altered as it alteration found. The whole obligation of the historian is to ascertain what mattered to men living at the time, to men who planned for their own day and not for posterity. To judge them and their deeds in the light of what will happen in the future may to some be sociology: it is assuredly not history.

66. B. Wilkinson in *Speculum*, xxxi (1956), 402: 'the loss [in 1422] by the Commons of most of the political initiative which they had held intermittently between 1376 and 1422 and which they were not to regain for more than two centuries'.

Appendix

THE KING'S PARLIAMENTS OF ENGLAND, 1258–1377

(For detailed reference to authorities, see *Trans. Royal Hist. Soc.*, 4th series, xi.172–75; *Bull. Inst. Hist. Research*, v.151–54, vi.85–88, viii.78–82. These lists, especially that for 1258–72, have been supplemented and amended in the light of later research. It should be added that 'London' and 'Westminster' are frequently used interchangeably. Where the evidence is absent, dubious, or conflicting, square brackets have been used.)

Year	Term	Place
1258	Easter	Westminster
	9 June	Oxford
	Michaelmas	Westminster
1259	Candlemas (2 February)	Westminster
	Easter	Westminster
	Michaelmas	Westminster
1260	Candlemas	London
	Easter	Westminster
	Midsummer	London
	Michaelmas	London
1261	23 February	London
	21 September	Windsor
1262	Candlemas	London
	Michaelmas	London
1263	8 September	London
	Michaelmas	London
1264	Midsummer	London

1265	Hilary	Westminster
	(13 January)	
	14 September	Winchester
1266	30 April	Northampton
	15 August	Kenilworth
1267	7 February	Bury St. Edmunds
	Martinmas	Marlborough
1268	July	Northampton
	Michaelmas	London
1269	Easter	London
	Midsummer	London
	Michaelmas	London
1270	Easter	Westminster
	July	Winchester
	Michaelmas	Westminster
1271	Michaelmas	Westminster
1272	Hilary	Westminster
	Michaelmas	Westminster
1275	Easter	London
	Michaelmas	Westminster
1276	Easter	Westminster
	Michaelmas	Westminster
1277	Easter	Westminster
1278	Easter	Westminster
	Midsummer	Gloucester
	Michaelmas	Westminster
1279	Easter	Westminster
	Michaelmas	Westminster
1280	Easter	Westminster
	Michaelmas	Westminster
1281	Easter	Westminster
	Michaelmas	Westminster
1283	Michaelmas	Acton Burnell
		(Shrewsbury)
1285	Easter	Westminster
	Michaelmas	Winchester
1286	[Easter	Westminster]
1289	Easter	Westminster
1290	Hilary	Westminster
	Easter	Westminster
	Michaelmas	Clipston
1291	Epiphany	Ashridge
	(7 January)	
1292	Epiphany	Westminster

1293	Easter	Westminster
	Michaelmas	Westminster
1294	[Hilary	London]
	Easter	Westminster
	Michaelmas	Westminster
1295	1 August	Westminster
	27 November	Westminster
1296	3 November	Bury St. Edmunds
1297	24 February	Salisbury
	Trinity	Westminster
	(8 July)	
	Michaelmas	London
1298	Easter	London
1299	Lent	Westminster
	Easter	Westminster
	Michaelmas	London
1300	Lent	Westminster
1301	Hilary	Lincoln
1302	Midsummer	Westminster
	Michaelmas	Westminster
1305	Lent	Westminster
	15 September	Westminster
1306	[Trinity	Westminster [1]]
	(30 May)	
1307	Hilary	Carlisle
	Michaelmas	Northampton
1308	Lent	Westminster
	Easter	Westminster
	Michaelmas	Westminster
1309	Easter	Westminster
	27 July	Stamford
1310	Candlemas	Westminster
1311	8 August	London
1312	20 August	Westminster
1313	Lent	Westminster
	Midsummer	Westminster
	23 September	Westminster
1314	9 September	York
1315	Hilary	Westminster
1316	Hilary	Lincoln
1318	Michaelmas	York

1. It is unfortunate that doubt should exist about the nature of this assembly, for it is the only one which women (i.e., the abbesses of Wilton, Winchester, Shaftesbury, and Barking) were summoned to attend.

1319	Easter	York
1320	Hilary	York
	Michaelmas	Westminster
1321	Midsummer	Westminster
1322	Easter	York
	14 November	York
1324	23 February	Westminster
	[20 October	Westminster]
1325	Midsummer	Westminster
	18 November	Westminster
1327	Hilary	Westminster
	Candlemas [2]	Westminster
1328	Candlemas	York
	Easter	Northampton
	Michaelmas	Salisbury
1329	Candlemas [3]	Westminster
1330	Mid-Lent	Winchester
	26 November	Westminster
1331	Michaelmas	Westminster
1332	16 March	Westminster
	9 September	Westminster
	4 December	York
1333	Hilary [4]	York
1334	Lent	York
	19 September	Westminster
1335	26 May	York
1336	Mid-Lent	Westminster
1337	3 March	Westminster
1338	Candlemas	Westminster
1339	Candlemas	Westminster
	Michaelmas	Westminster
1340	Hilary	Westminster
	Mid-Lent	Westminster
	12 July	Westminster
1341	Easter	Westminster
1342	–	–
1343	Easter	Westminster
1344	7 June	Westminster
1345	–	–
1346	11 September	Westminster
1347	–	–

2. An adjournment of the previous parliament.
3. An adjournment of the parliament at Salisbury.
4. An adjournment of the parliament in December 1332.

1348	Hilary	Westminster
	Mid-Lent	Westminster
1349	–	–
1350	–	–
1351	Candlemas	Westminster
1352	Hilary	Westminster
1353	–	–
1354	28 April	Westminster
1355	23 November	Westminster
1356	–	–
1357	Easter	Westminster
1358	Candlemas	Westminster
1359	–	–
1360	15 May	Westminster
1361	24 January	Westminster
1362	Michaelmas	Westminster
1363	Michaelmas	Westminster
1364	–	–
1365	Hilary	Westminster
1366	4 May	Westminster
1367	–	–
1368	1 May	Westminster
1369	3 June	Westminster
1370	–	–
1371	24 February	Westminster
1372	3 November	Westminster
1373	21 November	Westminster
1374	–	–
1375	–	–
1376	28 April	Westminster
1377	Hilary	Westminster

Glossary

(The definitions have been freed as far as possible from technicalities and do not pretend to cover all possible meanings.)

advowson: the right of presentation to a church or benefice.

afforcement of court: increasement in membership of court.

aid: payment to the king on specified occasions—his own ransom, the knighting of his eldest son, the marriage of his eldest daughter once—or to meet a special emergency.

alienation: transfer of rights of property to another.

amercement: payment made by wrongdoer who is 'in the mercy' of the court.

ancient demesne: land held by the Crown in the time of King Edward the Confessor (1043–66) and recorded in Domesday Book. *See* demesne.

assize: (i) rule or regulation; (ii) procedure in legal actions concerning land. See *darrein presentment, mort d'ancestor, novel disseisin, utrum;* (iii) itinerant court in which such actions were tried.

attainder: conviction of treason or felony and resulting in forfeiture of rights and property.

aula regis: the king's household court.

baron of exchequer: a judge of the court of the exchequer (*baron:* Old French for 'man').

barony: land held as a grant directly from the king.

bastardy: *See* special bastardy.

benefice: ecclesiastical appointment, with cure of souls, usually held by rector or vicar of parish church.

benevolence: tax imposed under guise of voluntary loan.

bill: (i) short, informal note; (ii) document initiating proceedings at common law or in equity; (iii) petition in parliament, on which enactment may be made. *See* petition.

carucage: tax on ploughland.

chamber: part of the king's household which dealt with his expenditure.

chancery: part of the king's household and responsible for writing his writs and other instruments of government.

Cinque Ports: originally 'Five Ports' like Sandwich on the southeast coast of England with special privileges.

common bench: court of common law, stationed at Westminster, to hear 'common pleas', i.e., actions between private individuals.

common law: law, originally unwritten, administered in royal courts, as distinct from local customary law, statute, or equity.

constitutions: ordinances.

convocation: synod of clergy of province of Canterbury or York.

coram rege: (i) taking place 'before the king' in his actual or fictitious presence; (ii) court of king's bench.

customs: (i) unwritten law; (ii) levies on imported or exported goods.

darrein presentment: action of 'last presentment' to discover the most recent patron of a church.

demesne: land held by king or lord for his own use. *See* ancient demesne.

disseisin: dispossession of land.

distress, distraint: seizure of chattels to enforce payment of debt or appearance in court, etc.

duress: force illegally used to compel someone to do something.

equity: rules supplementary to common law and administered usually in chancery.

escheat: reversion of property to feudal lord or Crown upon default of heir or upon conviction of treason or felony.

exchequer: (i) department for receiving and auditing Crown revenues; (ii) court of law, dealing particularly with actions involving such revenues.

excommunication: exclusion from communion of Church as method of enforcing judgements of church courts.

eyre: circuit of justices.

franchise. *See* liberty.

homage: acknowledgement by feudal tenant in return for his land that he is his lord's man (*homme*).

honour: scattered manors held by or under one lord.

hundred: district forming part of a county or shire.

inquest: investigation by means of sworn testimony.

justiciar: a high administrative and judicial officer who ruled for the king during his absence abroad and under him on his return.

king's bench: court of common law attendant on the king's person.

letters close: sealed and 'closed' letters, often enrolled on Close Rolls.

letters patent: sealed and 'open' letters, often enrolled on Patent Rolls.

liberty: (i) royal privilege granted to subject; (ii) area within which such privilege is enjoyed.

marriage: feudal right to arrange marriage of widow or ward.

mort d'ancestor: action to discover whether ancestor died in possession of land, thus validating his heir's succession.

movables: personal property that can be removed (as opposed to landed property), on which levies of taxation such as a tenth or a fifteenth were made.

novel disseisin: action concerning 'recent dispossession' of land unjustly and without judgement.

perambulation: delimitation of forest boundaries.

petition: (i) request, orally or in writing; (ii) written complaint presented to court of law, in particular to parliament. *See* bill.

plea: action at law, recorded on 'plea roll' of court.

praemunientes: clause in parliamentary writ of summons to bishops, 'requiring' them to summon to parliament representatives of the lower clergy.

proctor: equivalent in civil or canon law to attorney.

provisors: those holding papal 'provisions' or appointments to ecclesiastical office.

purveyance: exaction of provisions, especially for the king's household.

relief: payment to king or feudal lord on succession to property.

remembrancer: exchequer official who enrols memoranda 'for remembrance'.

roll: document, comprising parchment sheets, stitched end to end or all together at the top.

scutage: feudal payment in place of knight service in the field.

seisin: possession (often contrasted with ownership) of land.

serjeant-at-law: a senior barrister.

special bastardy: illegitimacy prior to parents' subsequent marriage.

spiritualities: ecclesiastical revenues, derived from tithes, etc. *See* temporalities.

staple: market with monopoly for sale of goods, especially wool.

subsidy: a grant of taxation in form of a carucage (*q.v.*), a tallage (*q.v.*), or scutage (*q.v.*); or on movables (*q.v.*); or by customs duties (*q.v.*).

synod: ecclesiastical council.

tallage: arbitrary levy, especially on property of unfree tenants and ancient demesne (*q.v.*) of Crown.

temporalities: secular possessions of ecclesiastics. *See* spiritualities.

tenant-in-chief: feudal tenant holding direct from the Crown.

tithe: a 'tenth' of produce, usually payable for maintenance of parochial clergy.

trailbaston: (i) offences by vagrants armed with cudgels; (ii) justices commissioned to try such offences; (iii) courts to hear and determine trespasses and wrongdoings throughout the country.

trespass: (i) criminal offence other than treason or felony; (ii) civil wrong, redressed by payment of damages.

utrum: an assize to discover 'whether' (*utrum*) land was held by lay fee or in fee alms, i.e., for spiritual services like praying for souls.

wardship: right of feudal lord to act as guardian during minority of heir.

waste: (i) uncultivated land; (ii) damage to property done by tenant.

watch and ward: the duty, especially in boroughs, to arrange day (ward) and night (watch) for the apprehension of those who break the peace.

writ: sealed document, transmitting an order from the king or his courts.

writ of course: a writ issued as matter of routine and requiring no special authority.

year book: reports of legal arguments in courts, usually common bench or eyre, and, with the invention of printing, published annually.

Bibliography

(So much has been written over the years upon parliament that this bibliography must be selective and concentrate in the main upon recent authoritative work on the subject. The attitude to bibliography, shown in the third edition of F. M. Stenton, *Anglo-Saxon England*, p. 723, has been rejected: namely, that books that do not agree with the author's contentions must be left out.)

Adams, G. B. *Council and Courts in Anglo-Norman England*. New Haven, 1926.

Annales Monastici. Ed. H. R. Luard. London: Rolls Series, 1864–69.

Baldwin, J. F. *The King's Council*. Oxford, 1913.

Barraclough, G. 'Law and Legislation in Medieval England', *Law Quarterly Review*, lvi (1940), 75–92.

Bémont, Charles. *Simon de Montfort*. Paris, 1884.

Blake, Robert. *The Unknown Prime Minister*. 1964.

Bracton, Henry. *Bracton's Note Book*. Ed. F. W. Maitland. London, 1887.

———. *De Legibus et Consuetudinibus Angliae*. Ed. G. B. Woodbine. New Haven, 1915–42; re-edited S. E. Thorne, Cambridge, Mass., 1966–

Brady, Robert. *Introduction to the Old English History*. London, 1684.

Britton. Ed. F. M. Nichols. Oxford, 1865.

Brown, A. L. 'The Commons and the Council in the Reign of

Henry IV', *English Historical Review*, lxxix (1964), 1–30.

Bury, J. B. *History of Freedom of Thought*. London, 1913.

Calendar Early Mayors' Court Rolls, 1298–1307. Ed. A. H. Thomas. Cambridge, 1924.

Calendar Irish Council Book, 1581–96. Ed. D. B. Quinn. Dublin, 1957.

Cam, H. M. 'From Witness of the Shire to Full Parliament', *Transactions Royal Historical Society*, 4th series, xxvi (1944), 13–33.

———. 'The Legislators of Medieval England', *Proceedings British Academy*, xxxi (1947), 127–50.

———. *Liberties and Communities in Medieval England*. Cambridge, 1944.

———. 'Mediaeval Representation in Theory and Practice', *Speculum*, xxix (1954), 347–55.

———. 'Stubbs Seventy Years After', *Cambridge Historical Journal*, ix (1948), 129–47.

———. 'The Theory and Practice of Representation in Medieval England', *History*, xxxviii (1953), 11–26.

Chaplais, Pierre. *The War of Saint Sardos*. London: Camden Society, 1954.

Chrimes, S. B. *English Constitutional Ideas in the Fifteenth Century*. Cambridge, 1936.

———. ' "House of Lords" and "House of Commons" in the Fifteenth Century', *English Historical Review*, xlix (1934), 494–97.

Clarke, M. V. 'Irish Parliaments in the Reign of Edward II', *Transactions Royal Historical Society*, 4th series, ix (1925), 29–62.

———. *Medieval Representation and Consent*. London, 1936.

Clementi, D. 'That the Statute of York of 1322 Is No Longer Ambiguous', in *Album H. M. Cam* (Louvain, 1962), ii.93–100.

Close Rolls, 1227–1272. London, 1902–38.

Commentaries of Pius II, Book III. Trans. by Florence A. Gragg, in Smith College Studies in History (Northampton, Mass.), vol. xxv (1939–40).

Curia Regis Rolls. London, 1923–

Davies, J. C. *Baronial Opposition to Edward II*. Cambridge, 1918.

Day, Mabel, and Steele, Robert. *Mum and the Sothsegger*. Oxford: Early English Text Society, 1936.

Deighton, H. S. 'Clerical Taxation by Consent, 1279–1301', *English Historical Review*, lxviii (1953), 161–92.

Denholm-Young, N. *The Country Gentry in the Fourteenth Century*. Oxford, 1969.

———. *Vita Edwardi Secundi*. London, 1957.

Dictionary of National Biography. London, 1885. Republished 1908–9.

Documents Illustrative of English History in the Thirteenth and Fourteenth Centuries. Ed. Henry Cole. London: Record Commission, 1844.

Dods Parliamentary Companion. London, 1970.

Dugdale, William. *Perfect Copy of the Summons of the Nobility to Great Councils and Parliaments.* London, 1685.

Dunham, W. H. *The Fane Fragment of the 1461 Lords' Journal.* New Haven, 1935.

Edwards, Sir Goronwy. 'The Commons in Medieval English Parliaments'. Creighton Lecture; London, 1958.

————. 'The Emergence of Majority Rule in English Parliamentary Elections', *Transactions Royal Historical Society,* 5th series, xiv (1964), 175–96, xv (1965), 165–87.

————. 'Historians and the Medieval English Parliament'. Murray Lecture; Glasgow, 1960.

————. 'Justice in Early English Parliaments', *Bulletin Institute Historical Research,* xxxvii (1954), 35–53.

————. 'The Personnel of the Commons in Parliament under Edward I and Edward II', in *Essays in Mediaeval History Presented to T. F. Tout* (Manchester, 1925), 197–214.

————. 'The *Plena Potestas* of English Parliamentary Representatives', in *Oxford Essays in Medieval History Presented to H. E. Salter* (Oxford, 1934), 141–54.

————. 'Some Common Petitions in Richard II's First Parliament', *Bulletin Institute Historical Research,* xxvi (1953), 200–213.

————. 'Taxation and Consent in the Court of Common Pleas, 1338', *English Historical Review,* lvii (1942), 473–82.

Ehrlich, Ludwig. *Proceedings against the Crown.* Oxford, 1921.

Ellis, Henry, ed. *Original Letters.* London, 1924–46.

Elsynge, Henry. *Expedicio Billarum Antiquitus: An Unpublished Chapter of the Second Book of the Manner of Holding Parliaments in England.* Ed. C. G. Sims. Louvain, 1954.

————. *The Manner of Holding Parliaments in England.* London, 1768.

Evans, E. 'Of the Antiquity of Parliaments in England: Some Elizabethan and Early Stuart Opinions', *History,* xxiii (1938), 206–21.

Fifoot, C. H. S. *Letters of F. W. Maitland.* London: Selden Society, 1965.

Foedera, Conventiones, Litterae, et Cujuscunque Generis Acta Publica. Ed. Thomas Rymer. London: Record Commission, 1816–69.

Fryde, E. B., and Miller, E. *Historical Studies of the English Parliament*. Cambridge, 1970. (A reprint of articles listed separately in this bibliography.)

Galbraith, V. H., ed. *The Anonimalle Chronicle*. Manchester, 1927.

Gesta Regis Henrici Secundi et Ricardi I. Ed. W. Stubbs. London: Rolls Series, 1867. (Now attributed to Roger of Howden.)

Gibb, Vicary, ed. *Complete Peerage of England, Scotland, Ireland, Great Britain, and United Kingdom*. London, 1910–59.

Glanvill. Ed. G. D. H. Hall. London, 1965.

Goodman, A. W., ed. *Chartulary of Winchester Cathedral*. Winchester, 1927.

Gray, H. L. *The Influence of the Commons on Early Legislation*. Cambridge, Mass., 1932.

Haas, Elsa de, and Hall, G. D. G. *Early Registers of Writs*. London: Selden Society, 1970.

Hale, Matthew. *Jurisdiction of the Lords House of Parliament*. London, 1796.

Harriss, G. L. 'The Commons Petitions of 1340', *English Historical Review*, lxxviii (1963), 625–54.

Haskins, G. L. 'Counsel and Consent in the Thirteenth Century', *Thought*, xv (1940), 247–67.

———. 'A Draft of the Statute of York', *English Historical Review*, lii (1937), 74–77.

———. *The Growth of English Representative Government*. Philadelphia, 1948.

———. 'The Petitions of Representatives in the Parliaments of Edward I', *English Historical Review*, liii (1938), 1–20.

———. *The Statute of York and the Interest of the Commons*. Cambridge, Mass., 1935.

———. 'Three Early Petitions of the Commonalty', *Speculum*, xii (1937), 314–18.

Hearne, Thomas. *Collection of Curious Discourses*. London, 1775.

Houghton, K. N. 'Theory and Practice in Borough Elections to Parliament during the Late Fifteenth Century', *Bulletin Institute Historical Research*, xxxix (1966), 130–40.

Howden, Roger of. *Chronica*. Ed. W. Stubbs. London: Rolls Series, 1868–71.

Hoyt, R. S. 'The Coronation Oath of 1308', *Traditio*, xi (1955), 235–57.

———. 'The Coronation Oath of 1308', *English Historical Review*, lxxi (1956), 353–83.

———. 'Recent Publications in the United States and Canada on the History of Representative Institutions before the French Revolution', *Speculum*, xxix (1954), 356–77.

––––––. 'Royal Demesne, Parliamentary Taxation, and the Realm', *Speculum*, xxiii (1948), 58–69.

––––––. 'Royal Taxation and the Growth of the Realm in Mediaeval England', *Speculum*, xxv (1950), 36–48.

Hurstfield, Joel. 'Was There a Tudor Despotism after All?', *Transactions Royal Historical Society*, 5th series, xvii (1969), 83–108.

Interim Report of the Committee on House of Commons Personnel and Politics, 1264–1832. London: H.M.S.O. (Cmd. 4130), 1932.

Jenkinson, H., and Fermoy, B. *Select Cases in the Exchequer of Pleas*. London: Selden Society, 1931.

Jolliffe, J. E. A. 'Some Factors in the Beginnings of Parliament', *Transactions Royal Historical Society*, 4th series, xxii (1940), 101–39.

Kantorowicz. E. H. *Laudes Regiae*. Berkeley, 1946.

Keeny, B. C. *Judgement by Peers*. Cambridge, Mass., 1949.

Kingsford, C. L. *The Song of Lewes*. Oxford, 1890.

Kirby, J. L. 'Councils and Councillors of Henry IV, 1399–1413' *Transactions Royal Historical Society*, 5th series, xiv (1964), 35–66.

Lander, J. R. 'The Yorkist Council and Administration, 1461 to 1485', *English Historical Review*, lxxiii (1958), 27–46.

Lapsley, G. T. *Crown, Community, and Parliament in the Later Middle Ages: Studies in English Constitutional History*. Ed. H. M. Cam and G. Barraclough. Oxford, 1951.

––––––. 'The Interpretation of the Statute of York', *English Historical Review*, lvi (1941), 22–51, 411–46.

Latham, L. C. 'Collection of the Wages of Knights of the Shire in the Fourteenth and Fifteenth Centuries', *English Historical Review*, xlviii (1933), 455–64.

Lewis, N. B. 'Re-election to Parliament in the Reign of Richard II', *English Historical Review*, xlviii (1933), 364-94.

Liber de Antiquis Legibus. Ed. T. Stapleton. London: Camden Society, 1846.

Liebermann, F. *Die Gesetze der Angelsachen*. Halle, 1903–16.

Lords Reports on the Dignity of a Peer. London, 1820–29.

Lowry, E. C. 'Clerical Proctors in Parliament and Knights of the Shire', *English Historical Review*, xlviii (1933), 443–55.

Lunt, W. E. 'The Consent of the English Lower Clergy to Taxation during the Reign of Henry III', in *Persecution and Liberty: Essays in Honor of G. L. Burr*. New York, 1932.

Lyon, Bryce. *Constitutional and Legal History of Medieval England*. New York, 1960.

McFarlane, K. B. 'Parliament and "Bastard Feudalism" ', *Transactions Royal Historical Society*, 4th series, xxvi (1944), 53–79.

McIlwain, C. H. *The High Court of Parliament and Its Supremacy*. New Haven, 1910; reprinted 1963.

——. 'Medieval Estates', *Cambridge Medieval History*, vii (1958), 664–715.

McKisack, May. *The Parliamentary Representation of the English Boroughs during the Middle Ages*. Oxford, 1932; reprinted 1961.

——. *The Fourteenth Century*. Oxford, 1959.

Madox, Thomas. *History and Antiquities of the Exchequer of England*, 2nd ed., London, 1769.

——. *See* Sims.

Maitland, F. W. *Collected Papers*. Cambridge, 1911.

——. *Records of the Parliament of 1305*, or *Memoranda de Parliamento*. London: Rolls Series, 1893; Introduction reprinted in *Maitland: Selected Essays* (Cambridge, 1937) and in *Select Historical Essays: Maitland* (Cambridge, 1957).

Marongiu, Antonio. *L'Istituto parlamentare in Italia*. 1949; revised and enlarged, 1962. Trans. with omissions and abbreviations in chapters and notes as *Medieval Parliaments: A Comparative Study*. (London, 1968).

Miller, Edward. 'The Origins of Parliament'. Historical Association Pamphlets; London, 1960.

Mirror of Justices. Ed. W. J. Whittaker, with Introduction by F. W. Maitland. London: Selden Society, 1893.

Mitchell, S. K. *Taxation in Medieval England*. New Haven, 1951.

Morris, W. A. 'Magnates and Community of the Realm in Parliament, 1264–1337', *Medievalia et Humanistica*, i (1943), 50–94.

Murimuth, Adam. *Continuatio Chronicarum*. Ed. E. M. Thompson. London: Rolls Series, 1889.

Myers, A. R. 'The English Parliament and the French Estates-General in the Middle Ages', in *Album H. M. Cam* (Louvain, 1962), ii.141–53.

——. 'A Parliamentary Debate of the Mid-Fifteenth Century', *Bulletin John Rylands Library* (Manchester), xxii (1938), 389–97.

——. 'Parliamentary Petitions in the Fifteenth Century', *English Historical Review*, lii (1937), 385–404, 590–613.

——. 'Some Observations on the Procedure of the Commons in Dealing with Bills in the Lancastrian Period', *University of Toronto Law Journal*, iii (1939), 51–73.

Neale, J. E. 'The Commons' Privilege of Free Speech in Parliament', in *Tudor Studies Presented to A. F. Pollard*, ed. R. W. Seton-Watson (London, 1924), 257–86.

Paris, Matthew. *Chronica Majora*. Ed. H. R. Luard. London: Rolls Series, 1872–84.

Parliamentary Writs and Writs of Military Summons. Ed. F. Palgrave. London: Record Commission, 1827–34.

Parry, C. H. *Parliaments and Councils of England*. London, 1839.

Pasquet, Désiré. *Essay on Origins of the House of Commons*. Paris, 1914; trans. Cambridge, 1925.

Perroy, Edouard. *Diplomatic Correspondence of Richard II*. London: Camden Society, 1933.

Petyt, William. *The Ancient Right of the Commons Asserted*. London, 1680.

Pike, L. O. *Constitutional History of the House of Lords*. London, 1894; New York, 1964.

Plucknett, T. F. T. 'Impeachment and Attainder', *Transactions Royal Historical Society*, 5th series, iii (1953), 145–58.

————. 'The Lancastrian Constitution', in *Tudor Studies Presented to A. F. Pollard*, ed. R. W. Seton-Watson (London, 1924), 161–81.

————. 'Parliament', in *The English Government at Work, 1327–1336*, ed. J. F. Willard and W. A. Morris (Cambridge, Mass., 1940), i.82–128.

————. 'The Place of the Council in the Fifteenth Century', *Transactions Royal Historical Society*, 4th series, i (1918), 157–89.

Pocock, J. G. A. *The Ancient Constitution and the Feudal Law*. Cambridge, 1957.

Pollard, A. F. 'The Clerical Organization of Parliament', *English Historical Review*, lvii (1942), 31–58.

————. *The Evolution of Parliament*. London, 1920; revised 1926.

————. 'Fifteenth-Century Clerks of Parliament', *Bulletin Institute Historical Research*, xv (1938), 137–61.

————. 'The Mediaeval Under-Clerks of Parliament', *Bulletin Institute Historical Research*, xvi (1939), 65–87.

————. 'Parliament in the War of the Roses'. Murray Lecture; Glasgow, 1936.

Post, Gaines. *Studies in Medieval Legal Thought: Public Law and the State, 1100–1322*. Princeton, 1964.

Powell, J. Enoch, and Wallis, Keith. *The House of Lords in the Middle Ages*. London, 1968.

Powicke, F. M. *King Henry III and the Lord Edward*. Oxford, 1947.

————. *The Thirteenth Century.* Oxford, 1953.

Proceedings and Ordinances of the Privy Council of England. Ed. N. H. Nicholas. London: Record Commission, 1834–37.

Prynne, William. *A Brief Register, Kalendar, and Survey of the Several Kinds and Forms of All Parliamentary Writs,* 4 vols. London, 1659–64. (The volume frequently cited as the *Brevia Parliamentaria Rediviva* is the third volume, bearing that distinct title.)

Ramsay, J. H. *History of the Revenue of the Kings of England.* Oxford, 1925.

————. *Lancaster and York.* Oxford, 1892.

Rayner, D. 'The Form and Machinery of the "Commune Petition" in the Fourteenth Century', *English Historical Review,* lvi (1941), 198–233, 549–70.

Red Book of the Exchequer. Ed. H. Hall. London: Rolls Series, 1896.

Register of John de Grandisson. Ed. F. C. Hingeston-Randolph. London: Canterbury and York Society, 1884–99.

Reich, A. M. *The Parliamentary Abbots to 1470.* Berkeley, 1941.

Richardson, H. G. 'The Commons and Medieval Politics', *Transactions Royal Historical Society,* 4th series, xxviii (1946), 21–45.

————. 'The English Coronation Oath', *Transactions Royal Historical Society,* 4th series, xxiii (1941), 129–58.

————. 'John of Gaunt and the Parliamentary Representation of Lancashire', *Bulletin John Rylands Library* (Manchester), xxii (1938), 3–50.

————. 'The Origins of Parliament', *Transactions Royal Historical Society,* 4th series, xi (1928), 137–83.

Richardson, H. G., and Sayles, G. O. 'The Clergy and the Easter Parliament, 1285', *English Historical Review,* lii (1937), 220–34.

————. 'The Earliest Known Official Use of the Term "Parliament" ', *English Historical Review,* lxxxii (1967), 747–50.

————. *The Early Statutes.* London, 1934.

————. 'The Exchequer Parliament Rolls and Other Documents', *Bulletin Institute Historical Research,* vi (1928–29), 129–55.

————. *Fleta.* London: Selden Society, 1955, 1973.

————. *Governance of Mediaeval England.* Edinburgh, 1963.

————. *The Irish Parliament in the Middle Ages.* Philadelphia, 1952; reprinted 1964.

————. 'The King's Ministers in Parliament under Edward I', *English Historical Review,* xlvi (1931), 529–50.

————. 'The King's Ministers in Parliament under Edward II', *English Historical Review,* xlvii (1932), 194–203.

————. 'The King's Ministers in Parliament under Edward III', *English Historical Review*, xlvii (1932), 377–97.

————. *Law and Legislation*. Edinburgh, 1966.

————. 'Parliamentary Documents from Formularies', *Bulletin Institute Historical Research*, xi (1934), 147–62.

————. *Parliament in Medieval Ireland*. Dublin: Historical Association, 1964.

————. 'The Parliament of Carlisle, 1307: Some New Documents', *English Historical Review*, liii (1938), 425–37.

————. 'The Parliament of Lincoln, 1316', *Bulletin Institute Historical Research*, xii (1935), 105–7.

————. *Parliaments and Great Councils in Medieval England*. London: Stevens, 1961.

————. 'The Parliaments of Edward I', *Bulletin Institute Historical Research*, v (1927–28), 129–50.

————. 'The Parliaments of Edward II', *Bulletin Institute Historical Research*, vi (1928–29), 71–85.

————. 'The Parliaments of Edward III', *Bulletin Institute Historical Research*, viii (1930), 65–82, ix (1931), 1–18.

————. 'The Provisions of Oxford', *Bulletin John Rylands Library* (Manchester), xvii (1933), 291–321.

————. *Rotuli Parliamentorum Anglie Hactenus Inediti*. London: Camden Society, 1934.

————. 'The Scottish Parliaments of Edward I', *Scottish Historical Review*, xxv (1928), 300–317.

————. *Select Cases of Procedure without Writ*. London: Selden Society, 1941.

Riess, Ludwig. *History of the English Electoral Law in the Middle Ages*. Leipzig, 1885; trans. by K. L. Wood-Legh, Cambridge, 1940.

Robbins, Caroline. 'Why the English Parliament Survived the Age of Absolutism', in *Studies International Commission for the History of Representative and Parliamentary Institutions* (Louvain, 1958), 179–213.

Rolls of Justices in Eyre for Yorkshire, 1218–19. Ed. D. M. Stenton. London: Selden Society, 1937.

Roskell, J. S. *The Commons and Their Speakers in English Parliaments, 1376–1523*. Manchester, 1965.

————. *The Commons in the Parliament of 1422*. Manchester, 1954.

————. 'Perspectives in English Parliamentary History', *Bulletin John Rylands Library* (Manchester), xlvi (1964), 448–75.

————. 'The Problem of the Attendance of the Lords in Medieval

Parliaments', *Bulletin Institute Historical Research*, xxix (1956), 153–204.

————. 'The Social Composition of the Commons in a Fifteenth-Century Parliament', *Bulletin Institute Historical Research*, xxiv (1951), 152–72.

Rothwell, H. 'Edward I and the Struggle for the Charters, 1297–1305', in *Essays in Medieval History Presented to F. M. Powicke*. Oxford, 1948.

Rotuli Litterarum Clausarum, 1204–1227. Ed. T. D. Hardy. London: Record Commission, 1833–44.

Rotuli Litterarum Patentium, 1201–1216. Ed. T. D. Hardy. London: Record Commission, 1835.

Rotuli Parliamentorum [1278–1503]. London, 1783.

Round, J. H. *Peerage and Pedigree*, especially the paper on 'The Origin of the House of Lords'. London, 1910.

Royal Letters of Henry III. Ed. W. W. Shirley. London: Rolls Series, 1862–66.

Rudishill, G. *See* Strayer.

Sayles, G. O. *The Medieval Foundations of England*. Methuen, 1948; Philadelphia, 1950.

————. 'Medieval Judges as Legal Consultants', *Law Quarterly Review*, lvi (1940), 247–54.

————. 'Parliamentary Representation in 1294, 1295, and 1307', *Bulletin Institute Historical Research*, iii (1925–26), 110–15.

————. 'Representation of Cities and Boroughs in 1268', *English Historical Review*, xl (1925), 580–85.

————. 'The Seizure of Wool at Easter 1297', *English Historical Review*, lxvii (1952), 543–47.

————. *Select Cases in the Court of King's Bench, 1272–1422*. 7 vols. London: Selden Society, 1936–71.

————. 'The Sources of Two Revisions of the Statute of Gloucester, 1278', *English Historical Review*, lii (1937), 467–74.

Sims, Catherine S. 'An Unpublished Fragment of Madox, *History of the Exchequer*', *Huntington Library Quarterly*, xxiii (1959), 61–94.

Smith, A. L. *Church and State in the Middle Ages*. Oxford, 1913.

Spufford, P. *Origins of The English Parliament*. London, 1967.

Stanley, A. P. *Historical Memorials of Westminster Abbey*, 5th ed. London, 1882.

Statutes of the Realm. London: Record Commission, 1810–28.

Steele. *See* Day

Stephenson, Carl. *Medieval Institutions*. Ithaca, 1954.

Strayer, J. R. 'The Statute of York and the Community of the Realm', *American Historical Review*, xlvii (1942), 1–22.

————, and Rudishill, G. 'Taxation and Community in Wales and Ireland, 1272–1327', *Speculum*, xxix (1954), 410–16.

Stubbs, W. *Constitutional History of England.* Oxford, 1896–97.

————. *Select Charters*, 9th ed., Oxford 1921.

Templeman, G. 'The History of Parliament to 1400 in the Light of Modern Research', *University Birmingham Historical Journal*, i (1948), 202–31; reprinted in R. L. Schuyler and H. Ausubel, *The Making of English History* (New York, 1952).

Thompson, Faith. *A Short History of Parliament, 1295–1642.* Minneapolis, 1953.

Thorgrimisson, T. 'Plenum Parliamentum', *Bulletin Institute Historical Research*, xxxii (1959), 69–82.

Tout, T. F. *Chapters in the Administrative History of Mediaeval England.* Manchester, 1920–33.

Treharne, R. F. 'The Nature of Parliament in the Reign of Henry III', *English Historical Review*, lxxiv (1959), 590–610.

Trueman, J. H. 'The Privy Seal and the English Ordinances of 1311', *Speculum*, xxxi (1956), 611–25.

————. 'The Statute of York and the Ordinances of 1311', *Medievalia et Humanistica*, x (1956), 64–81.

Unwin, George. 'The Estates of Merchants', in *Finance and Trade under Edward III*. Manchester, 1918.

Wedgwood, J. C., and Holt, A. D. *History of Parliament, 1439–1509: Biographies of Members of the Commons House.* London, 1936.

Wendover, Roger of. *Flores Historiarum.* Ed. H. O. Coxe. London: English History Society, 1841–44.

Weske, D. B. *Convocation of the Clergy.* London, 1937.

White, A. B. 'Some Early Instances of Concentration of Representatives in England', *American Historical Review*, xix (1914), 735–50.

————. 'Was There a "Common Council" before Parliament?', *American Historical Review*, xxv (1919), 1–17.

Wilkinson, B. 'The Coronation Oath of Edward II and the Statute of York', *Speculum*, xix (1944), 445–69.

————. *Studies in the Constitutional History of the Thirteenth and Fourteenth Centuries.* Manchester, 1937.

Willard, J. F. 'Edward III's Negotiations for a Grant in 1337', *English Historical Review*, xxi (1906), 727–31.

————. *Parliamentary Taxes on Personal Property, 1290–1334.* Cambridge, Mass., 1934.

Wood-Legh, K. L. 'The Knights' Attendance in the Parliaments of
    Edward III', *English Historical Review*, xlvii (1932), 398–413.
————. 'Sheriffs, Lawyers, and Belted Knights in the Parliaments
    of Edward III', *English Historical Review*, xlvi (1931), 372–88.
Year Book, 33–35 Edward I. Ed. A. J. Horwood. London: Rolls
    Series, 1879.

Index

(The names of modern historians have been printed in italics.)